# South Warn

# Memories

Recollections of growing up in a Hampshire village during the 1930-1950's.

A South Warnborough Memories Project

Published by the South Warnborough Memories Project

Contact: Ray Hillyer. Windrush, Lainston Close,
Dean Lane, Winchester,
Winchester, Hampshire,
SO22 5LJ
Email: Kayray@ntlworld.com

Sponsored By Hampshire County Council

Project Leader: Ray Hillyer
Cover Design: Leaf Hillyer

ISBN 0-9560302-0-7

Printed and Bound by RPM Print & Design,
2-3 Spur Rd, Quarry Lane, Chichester, West Sussex,
PO18 8PR

# Introduction

The idea for this book evolved, when I enquired into the possibility of getting my own story of growing up in South Warnborough in the 1930/50s, incorporated into the history of the village. From investigations, it soon became apparent that there was no such document or book recording those times.

Contact with the village, via Harriet Kennet, Clerk to the Parish Council, then started a year long project. It is with her enthusiasm and organisation that we have been able to get ex-villagers together, to write about their lives of those rather changing and turbulent times, of well over fifty years ago.

It must be emphasised that after this span of time, not all memories of an event, are identical or that any one contribution is necessarily in chronological order.

I started my story nearly two years before we embarked on this project and hence contains much more detail. The edited version, to suit our book, could apply to other young boys growing up in the village in that period.

Consequently, I wish it to be dedicated to our many friends from those days, who, for various reasons are not able to contribute.

Ray Hillyer

# South Warnborough Memories

# Contributors

# Margaret Appleby

Margaret Applebys recollection of South Warnborough 1945 to 1951

Our family was immigrants to South Warnborough. My father originated from Hull & my mother from Newcastle upon Tyne. Although my parents were of northern stock I regard myself as having a good deal of southerness in me as I was born in Romney Marsh, Kent in August, 1935, and lived in Hampshire until I was 15.

Our family's arrival in the village came about as a result of my father enlisting in the army at the outbreak of the Great War, where he was commissioned, but became one of the casualties at the Battle of the Somme in October, 1916. Eventually invalided out of service he went to Borneo and worked in the rubber industry but returned to England in 1925 suffering from ill-health due to his war injury. He remained in the south of the country receiving hospital treatment and taking casual work. My grandfather owned a paint and dye business in Hull but father never returned to the city.

My mother, who had emigrated to Australia when 19 years of age, came back to England in 1934 as the result of her father's death and the reading of the will. Her father was a dentist and property owner and the will was quite complex and the family large. She was returning to Australia, which she loved, when she and father met at an afternoon tea dance at The Ritz in London. From this meeting, she was determined to stay in this country and the rest, as they say, is history. Mother remained a 'Geordie' and came from a family of nine brothers and sisters, three of whom became dentists. The family name, Tinn, still exists in dentistry in the north.

We moved around in connection with my father's work and in the summer of 1945 arrived at South Warnborough village. He had taken employment as the Hunting Stables' Secretary for Mr. Frank Butler at Lees Hill Farm. I remember his wage was £3 per week with free accommodation, plus extra rations at harvest time. My mother took the job as caretaker for the Village Hall. Our family was accommodated in No I Lees Hill, and lived there until my father's death in February, 1951. He is buried in the churchyard of St. Andrew's Church. Mother and I were given four week's notice to quit the premises and it was decided we should go to Newcastle upon Tyne to live with her relatives. I lived there until after my marriage when we subsequently moved to Leeds, in connection with my police officer husband's work.

We are now grandparents with a son, who is a chemical engineer living with his family in London and a daughter, who is a secretary, living with her family in Leeds.

Mr. Brian Butler, the son, who lived at Greywell, was a prominent show jumper who competed at the White City. In the late 1940's he won the King George V Cup riding Tankard, the cup being presented to him by the Queen. The other principal show jumping horse he kept was called Brutus. The horses were all kept in the stables at Lees Farm and looked after by the groom, Mr. Cameron, who lived across the road from the farm. His daughter, Sheila, and I were good friends. Both keen knitters we used cardboard milk bottle tops to make pom-poms. With Mr. Brian Butler being a top show jumper, and friendly with many of the prominent contemporary show jumpers, I remember Colonel Harry Llewellyn and Pat Smythe visiting and chatting with my father.

Our cottage was the end one of three attached premises. The interior doors were somewhat small and the door lintels low and my father and mother were constantly suffering from bruises on their heads. The door into my parent's bedroom was so low they had to crouch to enter it. All doors had latches rather than handles. The windows were latticed with small diamond shaped panes, which seemed always to be loose and rattled in the wind, or fell out of the frame. The roof was thatched and the permanent home of a small menagerie of animals and creatures. Bats would come in through a window and birds and rodents took up occupancy in the straw. At night one could listen to the movements in the thatch and when this is by candlelight these sounds can become emphasised and a little unnerving! There were also numerous spiders. We had no electricity or gas and, in the early days, we had to walk to the well for water, which was next to the village pond. When darkness fell one gas lamp, numerous candles and the fire were our only sources of light. I wonder what modern Health and Safety officials would have to say bearing in mind the amount of timber and thatch in the property? Below is our house, which outwardly has not changed to this day.

The toilet was an outdoor chemical type, sited at the top of our garden. Two considerations came to mind when the need arose to visit it. What was the weather like? A visit in a light shower of rain was preferable to one in a thunderstorm and secondly, not to knock the walls or ceiling as this produced a shower of rust and small insects.

Mother used to bake and cook using the fire and an oven beside it until we were connected for electricity and father acquired a small Belling cooker. She bought yeast, etc. at the Co-op. Store in Odiham but never at the local Store as they would not sell anything on 'tic'. My father would not go into the local pub, because when he was ill my mother had requested a small quantity of brandy but they would only offer a full bottle, which she could not afford. Consequently, he took his custom to The Four Horseshoes at Long Sutton and the three of us would pay a visit on a Saturday evening. I always enjoyed a game of dominoes and other games with the landlord's children in a room at the back of the pub. A packet of crisps with the blue salt bag and a glass of lemonade would be sent through as refreshments.

Sometimes we would go to the cinema in Basingstoke or Odiham. A special treat I remember was a visit to Bertram Mill's Circus at Olympia. They had a flea circus and a notice at the exit saying '*Please return any of our artists who may have left with you as they are valuable*'! Once we went on holiday to Bournemouth where the highlight of the stay was when we visited 'Bobbys' Departmental Store. In the café a tempting selection of cakes was brought round and you were allowed to select just one. I chose the largest and creamiest and invariably suffered later as my stomach was not familiar with such richness. But I never resisted the temptation!

I remember most of the gardens in the village, which were well kept and cultivated a good supply of food for the householders. Ours was not heavily cultivated as father could not do hard physical work but he did grow some potatoes, onions, etc. I also remember picking orchids at the side of the footpath to Long Sutton. They were plentiful then, I wonder if they still are?

Both my parents smoked. Mother would smoke only Capstan or Players cigarettes but father grew his own tobacco plants in the back garden. He dried and then smoked the leaves in his pipe. Father also had a taste for curries, no doubt developed in the Far East and occasionally he would travel to London by train from Basingstoke to make a special purchase of the ingredients needed to make his 'specialities'.

The cottage at No 3 Lees Hill was occupied by

several prisoners-of-war when we moved in. For a while afterwards they continued to live there, working on the land. The ones from Italy would sing to us and I remember there being Irishmen as well. They were popular because they always had a good yarn to spin to us as well as telling us jokes. I think some were German but they kept to themselves. We girls would sit in the dark talking to them and it was all very exciting. One day they were all gone and that was the last we saw of them. I believe a bus arrived and took them away.

I attended Long Sutton Primary School, which had a solid fuel burning stove in the middle of the classroom, and then I went to Fairfields School in Basingstoke where I gained the distinction of a nil mark for punctuality of attendance for my schooldays!

This was because the bus from South Warnborough to Basingstoke always arrived after the school had started and I found myself, together with a few others who must have had a similar bus service, having to stand outside the assembly hall to await the ending of morning assembly.

The bus driver operated in the true rural tradition, stopping, in addition to the designated bus stops, wherever a person signalled their intention to travel with him. If I was late getting ready the driver would stop and toot his horn and I would have to scramble my things together and run down the road to get on the bus! I remember, the favourite driver was Freddie and the girls would try to get the seat next to him when he was driver, as he used to sing to us. After school I had a half hour wait for the bus home. I would buy a Chelsea bun and eat it before the 50 minutes ride on the bus until I was dropped off at the village. Most homework was done on the bus (producing comments from teachers about by handwriting). At home' Dick Barton - Special Agent' was never missed at 6.15pm, listened to on an accumulator powered Pye radio.

The nearest airfield to the village was Odiham. I remember the barrage balloons which surrounded the airfield and, at that time, wondering how the men who had to man them got into them! I used to see and hear the aircraft but never knew much about them.

My father had responsibility for collecting the milk yield returns from the dairy farm in North

Warnborough and I would accompany him on his round in an old MG car, which took us past the watercress beds. These beds were occasionally visited by me and my friends on our bicycles when 'samples' would be brought home for tea. I remember the bats which live in the tunnel at Greywell. (2008 – it has been a protected site for bats over many years). He also took the car to collect bits of machinery, as required, and during school holidays I could accompany him, which was a bit of a treat as very few persons in the village owned a car.

The cows all had names, several of them Margaret after me, Margaret 1, Margaret 2, etc., of which I was very proud. At milking time they all went to their allocated stall in the byre, any cow that got into the wrong stall was quickly removed from it by the rightful owner. Milking was by machines whilst the cows were the picture of contentment munching the feed provided for them. The only animal I was wary of was a bull called Ferdinand the Second. He used to 'dance' when he saw us approaching. Father would go in beside him and rub his ears but I never lost my healthy sense of respect for the beast as he was, to my eyes, huge. I never asked what happened to Ferdinand the First!

Father, mother and I used to cycle to Alton on a

Saturday and have a cup of tea in the cafe but father would occasionally go cycling alone and I recall him commenting once about stopping at the home of and talking to Field Marshall Montgomery at Isington, near Froyle. There was a back road which was more or less a direct route to Isington.

When I first arrived in the village I was conscious that all the children seemed to have a bicycle. I did not have one and had to walk or run everywhere. One day, however, my father told me to accompany him to the farm, where he produced for me my first bicycle. It was a lady's model, obviously very old, with the u shaped crossbar and had been repainted. The rear wheel had a covering of netting to stop a skirt becoming entangled in the spokes. I suppose I had, in father's estimation, now grown tall enough to be able to ride it and ride it I did, everywhere. I cannot remember the make but it was certainly durable as I rode it continuously until we left the village.

There was no entertainment other than the radio, so we children had to be imaginative, resourceful and sociable. An abundance of chalk in the garden meant we could quickly map out courts and lines for hop scotch, etc. We would meet by the pond at the foot of the "Cross Tree". Occasionally there was entertainment when a dance would be held in the village hall and sometimes an amateur dramatics group would put on a play or, at Christmas, a pantomime.

Christmas time was very traditional, with the dinner; listening to the King's Christmas broadcast and presents. I remember receiving books which very clearly second hand as I would find that the puzzles had been completed! Not daunted I used to erase the pencilled in answers and then complete them myself. The church choir, in which I sang, used to sing carols around the village.

Village life was very calm and quiet compared to modem times. We children would meet by the pond at the foot of the village, play, talk and compete at doing summersaults on

the railings surrounding the pond.

There was a large tree in the centre of the road junction, next to the pond, and that was the main rendezvous point for us. The tree was ancient and hollow inside so cement had been placed in the trunk to keep it standing. I remember a kingfisher being on the pond so there must have been fish in it. Occasionally there would be a dance in the village hall and sometimes an amateur dramatics group would put on a play and at Christmas a pantomime. When my mother cleaned the hall, friends and I would sometimes go in and try on costumes, which were kept under the stage for the amateur dramatics. Otherwise we had to be imaginative and resourceful in filling in our spare moments. Whist drives were a popular evening with the adults.

I was friendly with Daphne James, who lived at Long Sutton. Her father was a teacher at the Lord Wandsworth Agricultural College. We sat together on the school bus. I always looked forward to the end of term dance, to which I would be invited, and was held at the college. This was the opportunity for the boys to dress smartly and the girls to put on their finest. I only occasionally got some new clothes, when father received his war pension cheque. For one particular dance I did not possess a new dress so Mother came to the rescue and proved her resourcefulness by somehow acquiring a parachute from which she fashioned a dress for me. In my new designer silk dress with a cummerbund I felt I was the belle of the ball! At that time I wonder how many parachutes ended up in the hands of dressmakers? Its alluring effect must have worked as I was invited to dance several times by the same boy, Peter Plumley!

Seasonally our time was constructively filled for us. Potato planting and later, the picking, took place at Butler's farm at Dogmersfield, where fruit was also grown. Loganberries were a speciality and I loved helping my parents to pick them! Fruits of the hedgerow were a special treat. Walnuts were collected from parkland off Froyle road and pickled. Blackberries were always welcome and together with windblown apples, they were made into lovely pies.

Rabbit pie was a regular dish whether roast, stewed, fricasseed, boiled or casseroled, it often appeared on the menu. Our cat was particularly adept at catching them and they were numerous in the pre-myxomatosis days. The cat, which was a big one, would kill and bring a rabbit into the house and so more than earned its keep. The same cat would allow me to dress it in doll's clothes, after which it would sleep contentedly in the doll's pram, or be taken for a walk!

We also kept a capon in a coop in the garden for Christmas and when it was the right size it also went into the pot.

I kept pet rabbits in a hutch at the top of the garden but one night the inevitable happened, a fox broke in and killed every one of them. None were taken or eaten, just killed and left. I suppose the fox thought of it as adding to its larder but to me it was just another reason why the hounds should catch it. There was a local Hunt which met about once a month in front of the public house, then called The Plough Inn. In their red coats they made a spectacle with their magnificent horses and the pack of hounds. We followed them on our pedal cycles wherever possible and they always had a good following support, some on foot and some in vehicles. I don't remember that they caught all that many foxes, (maybe they did), but it was an exciting community event at which, it seemed, most of the village attended on a hunting day. Cries of 'tally-ho' could be heard around the village.

Gymkhana time was exciting. It was held in early summer in the field next to Lees Hill Farm. Horses and ponies from the surrounding area would compete with their riders for the status that came with the winning rosette. Lots of horseboxes and some ponies and traps came to the event. Harvest time was always a busy time and it was a case of many hands made light work. We somehow all managed to do our bit to help get it in. I'm not sure whether or not the Butlers owned or used a combine harvester but I remember the two horses, Punch and Judy pulling a flat cart stacked with straw. We delighted in riding on this. There was some kind of mill at the foot of the village and I recall watching as the grain trickled down into bags when it was working. It may have been a threshing machine or just a granary. Straw in bales was brought in from the fields and stored in the big barn next to the stables at Lees Farm. 'John the Thresher' would come and thresh the cereals .He lived and slept in a wooden hut until the threshing was completed and then moved on

There were 'prefabs' at the top of the village. The Spreadborough and Spivey families lived there. George Spreadborough and a brother lived in the village but their brother was a policeman in London, I remember they were all physically big men. The Spivey family originated from South Africa and Evelyn Spivey was a friend of my mother. There was a mother and three daughters.

The village policeman lived opposite the pub and used to patrol his beat on a bicycle. We only ever incurred his wrath if he caught us in the act of pinching the vicars' apples! He would drop his bike and pretend to chase us, we scattered! The vicar had a large orchard and, accessing it by a wooden door next to the pond. We children used to sneak in and held ourselves to an apple or pear. His wife always managed to appear as if she had pushed her face into a bag of flour before leaving home! I cannot imagine her ever becoming suntanned.

Life was a bowl of cherries. I loved living in the village, knew everyone and everyone knew me. I liked school, had lots of friends and loved my schoolwork, particularly English. Mr. Nichol was the English teacher, an excellent teacher if a bit short tempered. I later learned he had been injured in the war and had a steel plate in his head, which possibly accounted for his mood swings.

Christmas 1950 was over and I had enjoyed it, especially the brand new books that father gave me. This Christmas I did not have to rub out someone else's answers. The Christmas apple and orange were there as usual. Father also gave me a card and invited me to choose and write on it the location at which we would spend our summer holidays. (When I continued the custom of an apple and orange with my own children they suggested it should be several oranges and a pound of apples! (times have changed).

When I left for school that Thursday I saw my father was lying on a make-up bed in the sitting room, he appeared to be asleep. Mother said he was not very well and would not be going to work that day. I went off to school and forgot about circumstances at home. After school I bought my usual Chelsea bun and went to wait the half hour for the 'bus. The weather was very cold and it seemed it might snow. The 'bus stop was outside the cinema. In those days the cinema showed the same film all week and the hoardings showed stills from the film, with close up pictures of the stars. Often there were pictures of James Mason and Phyllis Calvert and it seemed always Stewart Grainger, who was my favourite. I was so engrossed in viewing that I did not realise my 'bus was there and seemed to be driving off; at least five minutes before time. I ran like hell and banged on the door, which opened and I got in. The driver was a stranger to me. He said he was new to the route as a lot of people were off with the flu. (By the time I returned home my thoughts were, he was new to driving and would be better employed on a tractor). Several times he took a wrong road and at one point the road was too narrow and he had to reverse. At Upton Grey cross roads he was going to go straight on and miss the village out. I told him the next ‘bus was not until tomorrow, persons could be waiting for this one. I offered to sit on the front seat to direct him and keep him on the correct route to South Warnborough. He grudgingly agreed and moved his ticket machine onto the floor. We arrived home in record time, five minutes early! He asked where the ‘bus stop was and I pointed out the tree, adding the driver usually stopped and let me off outside my house. He continued on to the tree.

I ran into the house and straight into the sitting room to see my father. He was not there. The folding bed was still there; no fire, the fire place was cleaned out and a clean piece of newspaper in it, like during the summer. I nearly collided with my mother coming from the kitchen. “You are early” she said. “Yes, a different driver. Where is my father? Is he is hospital?” She said “Sit down whilst I make you a cup of tea. I have some very sad news. You know I was going to ask the doctor from Odiham to call in because your dad was ill. The doctor could not get here in time”. “He can’t be dead, he was alive this morning” was all I could say.

My mother then said the undertakers from Odiham had taken father’s body to their Funeral Parlour as our cottage was too small to house the coffin. The coffin was to be returned to the village on the following Thursday and mother suggested I may prefer to stay away from the church service as a lot of people would be there, father being well liked in the village. She said she would make a light tea and mourners could call at the cottage, with possibly me in charge of the refreshments. She then suggested I go and see if I could find any of my friends.

That weekend our cottage was awash with sadness, mother and I there alone. I remember asking her if we could take rooms nearer school so I could arrive on time. She told me we would put our furniture in storage and stay with relatives. I responded by saying "We do not have any relatives around here". She then explained we would be going to stay with a relative in Newcastle upon Tyne.

It seemed like a million miles away. Recollecting visits to the North East a couple of times I said "We cannot live there; I cannot understand what they say"! I felt as if I had to leave my whole world. Mother's only comment was to the effect I was young and would soon settle down. When I did get to Newcastle my cousins accused me of speaking 'posh'.

On the Monday mother went to Basingstoke. She asked me if I wanted to stay at home for the day but I opted to go to school as the house would be too quiet. We travelled on the 'bus together. She had made a number of telephone calls from a friend's house as we did not have the telephone. On the Tuesday the undertakers came to make final arrangements. At the time I did not, but now do, realise what a disruption to our lives had occurred and it so suddenly. And the only help available was from friends and relatives.

On the day of the funeral my mother was up early making cakes and sandwiches. Some friends came and helped her. I stayed at home and prepared for the mourners who eventually arrived, including the undertaker and his assistant. These gentlemen were dressed entirely in black; the undertaker wearing a stovepipe hat with ribbons. They seemed to be persistently standing next to me throughout their stay. They kept talking to me and I am sure they were being sympathetic but I was somewhat in awe of them and found their appearance and presence very unnerving. I was pleased to see them go.

About three weeks after father's death an enormous Holt's Furniture van arrived to remove our furniture. It was not that we had a lot but that they did not have a small enough van.

We travelled north by train, taking my father's cat, Mickey, with us. It travelled in the guard's van, was ill upon arrival, taken to the vets and promptly died.

Mother went to stay with a sister and I went to my uncle's house. He was a dentist living in a large house near the sea with his wife and my two cousins, a boy and a girl. My cousin, Terrence, has just retired as a dentist and his sister's husband was also a dentist, so it remained a family occupation. My aunt, who was very involved with the theatre as an amateur, used to go shopping in a mink coat! They had an electric Bendix washing machine and the pantry was full of tinned fruit and Carnation Milk, which I adored. It was a different world and I thought it was wonderful. There was even a flush toilet! And so I entered another world.

My uncle suggested I go to the Lambert Commercial College at North Shields, which he arranged and paid the fees for me to attend. He was a very generous and kind man. I stayed with the family for about eight months and then got employment with a Newcastle firm called Tyne Brand Products. Mother and I moved into a property in Jesmond, living on the upper floor and renting out the lower floor and basement. I became the secretary for the Northern Manager for Electrolux, met my husband-to-be at a dance and so the story continued.

Although force of circumstance has meant I have lived in urban areas for much of my life, given an option, I should not have missed, for anything, my happy, formative, years in rural South Warnborough and still get immense pleasure from revisits when we are in the south. May it remain as unspoiled and pleasant as it is, for generations to come.

# Margie Adlam

In 1935 my Mum and Dad, Elsie and George Adlam moved down to South Warnborough from Hampton Hill, near London, with Rene who was born at Notting Hill and Roy born at Hampton Hill. Rene was 14years older than me and Roy is 7 years older.

I'm Margery (Margie) the baby of the family. I was born in South Warnborough in 1936 at Greenacres, the house that stands next to the footpath, by the side of what used to be the Vicarage and opposite the pub.

This is me at 4 months old

(not my best kept photo!)

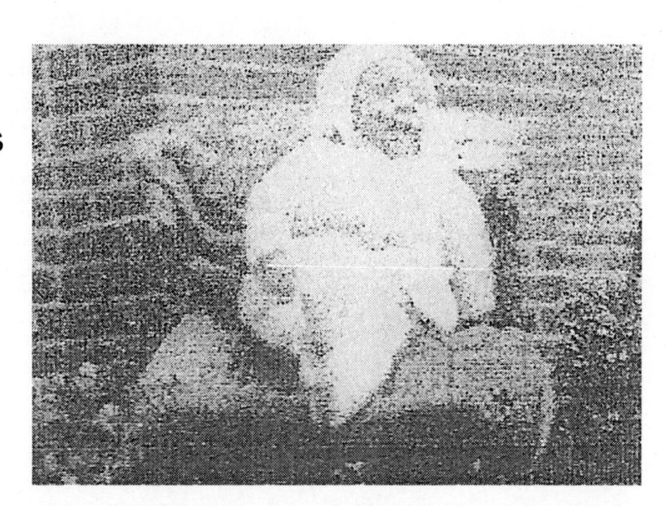

I started school at South Warnborough, not that I can recall much of the time there, except for one day when the nurses came to give us injections. I took one look at them and screamed really hard. Then I ran all the way home and locked myself into the toilet and would not come out! I don't think I went back to school that day!

This is me and a few recognizable faces at the school in 1941/42

Then it was of to Long Sutton School followed by Buryfields School in Odiham. I just do not remember much of my schooldays, probably because I hated school! I do remember taking the exam for the Gregg Secretarial College in Southampton two years running and passing both times, but I decided that was not what I wanted to do.

Growing up in South Warnborough was great and we had a lot of fun with plenty to do. Mum and Dad had a large garden with lots of space, so we had rabbits, chickens and a goat.

There were quite a few girls of my age, so we used to hang out together, including Helen Knight,

Joy Oliver, Ann Hillyer and Sheila Cameron. To this day we still see a lot of each other.

This photo is of Ann, Helen, Joy and me against the Vicarage wall.

Before I left school, I was helping to look after Annabel Nickisson and after I left school I became her nanny. Sheila was nanny to Thomas Butler and Joan Goodchild was nanny to Harriet Guy. We had some great times together - taking our charges for walks, going to each others parties, taking Annabel to her dancing class in Farnham and going on holiday with the family.

When I reached sixteen Mum and Dad decided I could train to be a Nursery Nurse. I had an interview at County Hall, London and was accepted. I began my training at a nursery with children 0-5 years in Dorking, Surrey. It was a very happy time in my life, except during my 3-years, my Dad died. I went home for 3 to 4 weeks to be with my Mum and afterwards I caught rheumatic fever, thereby missing about 2 months of my training.

During this period I had a boyfriend, Jim Digweed, brother of Vi, married to my brother Roy. Jim was doing his National Service, including periods in Germany and Malaya.

When my training was finished all I wanted to do was to get married. Jim completed his time in the army and we made arrangements to get married at South Warnborough church in 1956. We then went to live in a house at Powntley Copse for a year, before moving to Basingstoke and later in 1974, we moved to Old Basing.

# Roy Adlam

Here is an early school photograph of Roy William, probably taken at South Warnborough School

The photo below shows the whole school with Mrs. Bowie, the only teacher. Roy is there with Ray and their many friends.

Here we are as a family outside of our new home, which was called Green Acres, and is opposite the Plough Inn. Unfortunately, my big sister Irene (known as Rene) is partially hidden by part of the garden rustic work.

My younger sister Margie is in my mothers arms.

For interest I've included the statement for the cost of the house, built in 1935.

Also - Sections of the plans as used by the builders.

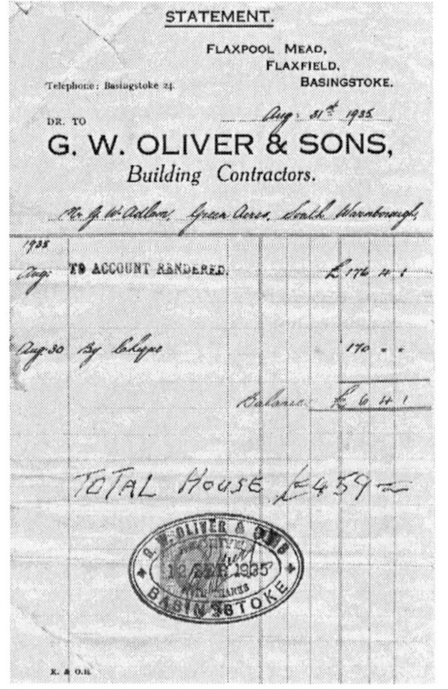

STATEMENT.

Telephone: Basingstoke 24.

FLAXPOOL MEAD,
FLAXFIELD,
BASINGSTOKE.

DR. TO Aug: 31st 1935

G. W. OLIVER & SONS,
*Building Contractors.*

Mr. G. W. Adlam, Green Acres, South Warnborough

| 1935 | | |
|---|---|---|
| Aug: | TO ACCOUNT RENDERED. | £176 14 1 |
| Aug 30 | By Cheque | 170 " " |
| | Balance | £6 14 1 |

TOTAL House £459 —

G. W. OLIVER & SONS
RECEIVED
12 SEP 1935
BASINGSTOKE

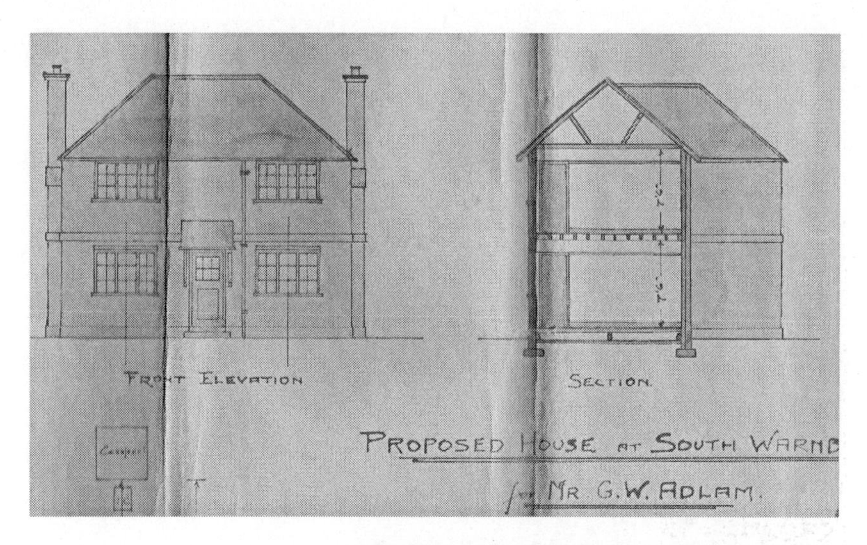


My mother's ration book and note that the date is eight years after the end of WW2, when so many foods were still strictly rationed.

R.B.1 16
1
SERIAL NO.
MINISTRY OF FOOD
1953-1954
BA 216417
RATION BOOK
Surname ADLAM Initials (ELSIE) M
Address
IF FOUND RETURN TO ANY FOOD OFFICE
F.O. CODE No.

6 ENTER NAMES AND ADDRESSES
MEAT
EGGS
FATS
CHEESE
BACON
SUGAR
SPARE

At weekends we would go to the local farm to help with the haymaking. Here I am walking with a

carthorse and wagon in the hayfield.

I remember that after helping on the farm we would sometimes go into the barn to smoke cigarettes, as most of the boys did at that time!! Unfortunately, on one occasion the hay in the barn caught fire and the barn was badly damaged. My Dad had to pay for the damage caused and I was not allowed out for a week!!

When I was a little older, I joined in the South Warnborough Church activities and became a choirboy. I loved to sing and I also learnt to ring the church bells.

I did my secondary schooling at Long Sutton School and left the school when I reached the age of 14. I was immediately able to start a 5-year apprenticeship as a vehicle mechanic with W. W. Webber in Basingstoke. Afterwards, I went into the Army for 2 years National Service.

Motorcycling

During my early years I became very friendly with Owen Tyler who owned the garage in the village. Owen taught me how to ride a motorcycle and at the age of just sixteen, helped me to enter the world of scrambling. Here I am after an event, with both my motorcycle and myself splattered with snow! (a very old newspaper cutting)

## My Social Life

One of my other interests was dancing and I went to the local dances held regularly on Saturday nights at the Village Hall.

It was there that I met Violet, my future wife. I was 22 years old when I left the village to get married.

## Emigration

After a short period Vi and I decided to emigrate to Australia. In those days it meant a six-week journey by sea.

Before we left we had a lovely party with family and friends at the Village Hall. Here we are enjoying the occasion - notice the band at the back?

We lived in Australia for three years before returning home to Basingstoke. It was there we started our own business named “Roy Adlam Motors”. I was then able to continue with my hobby of racing motorcycles and I eventually became the Southern Centre Champion.

We still love to visit South Warnborough, when I can relive the happy memories of my earlier life growing up in the village.

# Sheila Cameron

**I** was born at Peacock Cottage, now called "Up Steps", opposite the Village Hall in South Warnborough on January 2nd 1936.

My father Bert Cameron, after leaving the army and marrying my mother, came to South Warnborough in 1934 where he became groom for Mrs. McClean, who lived at The Lodge. They later moved to Bentley, where my brother Kevin was born.

In 1942, the family moved back to South Warnborough to live at Lees Farm Cottage and where my father went to work for Mr. Frank Butler. They started a very successful Stud Farm and Show Horse Stables at which Brian (Frank's son) and my father won many prizes.

My sister Valetta was born at Lees Farm and also 20 years later, our baby brother Andrew.

Growing up in South Warnborough was a happy time and as our house was in the stable yard, we had a lot of freedom. We kept dogs, cats, chicken, rabbits and also a donkey called Enoch that threw us off if we tried to ride it. Enoch would get out at night and roam the village, so Dad was always looking for him.

We also had a pet lamb which we would take to Horse Shows to collect money for charity. For a while we looked after RAF Odiham's mascot goat.

I went to the village school in South Warnborough and then on to Long Sutton school. From there I went to Alton until the Aldershot and District buses stopped running, and then had to finish my last year or two at Odiham.

My best friend was and still is Margery Adlam, who lived opposite "The Plough" pub and my other friend was Mary Evans (Loader) who lived along Ford Lane (Gastons Lane). We were all in the Church Choir and at that time the vicar was Rev. Oldfield.

Here we are, with the Pony Club, outside of the Church. I am with Margery, Mary Evans and my sister Valetta.

SUNDAY MORNING: RIDERS GO TO SERVICE AT A COUNTRY CHURCH

Members of a pony club who were camping in Hampshire attended morning service at the picturesque parish church of South Warnborough. They rode to church and back to camp.

We played with the local boys when they were short of players for cricket and sometimes rounders. To name a few, there was George Spreadborough, John Hillyer, Tommy Goodchild, Roland Gabriel (the local bobby's son) and Roley White, who I later married.

Then we all suddenly left school and went out to work and later the boys went off to do their National Service, to return as grown men! We girls then saw them in a different way!

I started going out with Roley White and we married at St. Andrews on 18th July 1959. We had 30 happy years until Roley passed away in 1990.
After we married, we moved to Basingstoke for a few years and then to Old Basing, where I have lived for 39 years. Margie and I are still good friends and she lives just up the road from me.

South Warnborough has changed a lot, with new houses built on every piece of spare ground and everyone is a stranger.

**I suppose this is progress**??!!

# Roland Gabriel

**M**y life in South Warnborough began in1941at the age of 6, when my father who was a policeman moved from Selbourne to replace the then current policeman, PC Davis, who was being enlisted into the armed forces

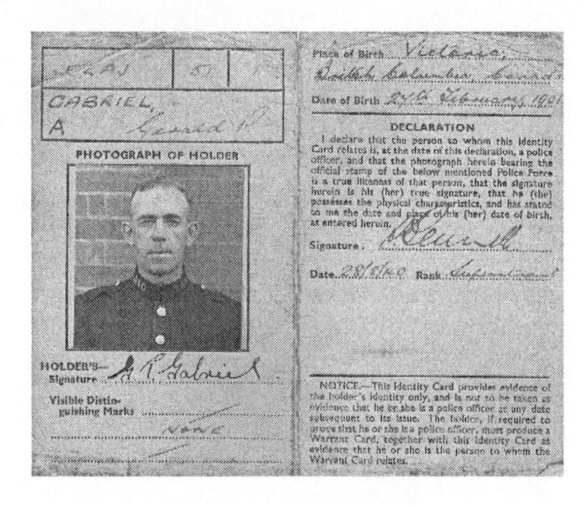

GABRIEL,
A

PHOTOGRAPH OF HOLDER

HOLDER'S—Signature

Visible Distinguishing Marks NONE

Place of Birth

Date of Birth

DECLARATION

I declare that the person to whom this Identity Card relates is, at the date of this declaration, a police officer, and that the photograph herein bearing the official stamp of the below mentioned Police Force is a true likeness of that person, that the signature herein is his (her) true signature, that he (she) possesses the physical characteristics, and has stated to me the date and place of his (her) date of birth, as entered herein.

Signature

Date Rank

NOTICE.—This Identity Card provides evidence of the holder's identity only, and is not to be taken as evidence that he or she is a police officer at any date subsequent to its issue. The holder, if required to prove that he or she is a police officer, must produce a Warrant Card, together with this Identity Card as evidence that he or she is the person to whom the Warrant Card relates.

A copy of my fathers warrant card – would he put fear into the boys of the village? (and maybe into some of the older would-be-scoundrels!!)

I was enrolled into the school in the village where the headmistress was Mrs Ball, who, as I remember was a tall, stark rather severe lady. One of the games some of us boys enjoyed, was to make mud balls and throw them at the wall of the school to stick. Another recollection was when we were taken on what was known as "nature walks" along Gaston Lane. I think it was those walks that gave me a lasting interest for the countryside.

Towards the end of my time at the village school I acquired a jackdaw from one of the Charlton boys who lived at New Farm. This bird was quite a character and would spend time with Mr. Duce one of the roadmen, pecking about in his barrow, as well as visiting other villagers. At times it would terrorise the school children and not let them out of school! One boy Jimmy Spreadborough, would come and ask my mother to remove the bird so they could get out. Another roadman – Mr. Smith lived next door to us. (His son was an "earlier lad" of the village, who had left to join the army). His wife had rather a bushy beard, and as a youngster, when I first saw it, I could hardly take my eyes off it. Alas, my jackdaw took a dislike to her and would peck her. It mysteriously disappeared and we all had our suspicions!!

I then went to Long Sutton School where the headmaster was a Mr. Wilmott.

Here is one of my school photos and when my friends saw it, they said I was just like my Dad?

It was an enjoyable time there. We had gardens which we

tended and the more senior boys did woodwork. (I don't remember the other lessons so clearly) At lunch times our sport included playing chase in the trees at the side of the school (I don't think the health and safety rules would allow that sort of game now!

In the summer, some of the time was spent getting a lift into the harvest field with Arthur Knight, who used to bring in the corn to the dryer from the combine harvester. I think Butlers were the first to have one of these "modern" machines which was driven by Archie Harris, and against all health and safety rules of today, he would let us have a ride with dust and bits flying everywhere. One of the perks of harvest time was catching rabbits that ran out of the corn. We would chase the unfortunate animals with long sticks and if we succeeded in catching one, it would make a tasty meal as rationing was still in place.

When I was a bit older, I got a job with Mr "Chico" Yalden from Long Sutton. Jimmy Spreadborough and I were allowed to drive his tractors. Jimmy was the lucky one – he had the Ford Major! We had trailers which were stacked with sheaves of corn to be taken back to the rick. It was amazing to me how, another Yalden by the nickname of Plucky would look at the area of a field and then mark out the exact base size of the rick needed, a skill which I would think has now died out.

I left Long Sutton School to go to Amery Hill in Alton for the remainder of my schooldays and on leaving became a dental mechanic (as it was then called) to Mr. Kynoch in Basingstoke. There were no buses so I cycled each way to work until I was old enough to get my first motorbike.

Whilst writing this a lot of memories come flooding back. All of us seemed to enjoy life and have fun with simple things like getting tyres from Owen Tyler and using them as hoops to roll down Lees Hill to the main road - very little traffic about in those days!! Another pastime was sliding on the village pond in the winter - if the ice gave way and your feet got wet, the smell was awful! One winter there was prolonged frost, so we all went sledging in one of Butler's fields.

Some of us joined the church choir, when we got the princely sum of 3d for Sundays. The church was lit by oil lamps and bats would flit about inside during the service! Mr. Ash would ring the bells and I remember him gritting his teeth while doing so! Mr. Oldfield was the rector. One of our perks was that the boys would be taken to the Farnborough Air Show by a member of the congregation (his name escapes me after so many years). My mother played the organ in the church for some years and also played at some of the local weddings.

Christmas was another highlight when the choir went carol singing. At first we went on a horse-drawn cart driven by Mr. Hall who was the handyman at Blounce - he was also a Special Constable and was quite good at chasing the lads!!

On the tour of the village we got many goodies, i.e. mince pies and liquid refreshment, especially at the large houses – making it well worth the chilly trip!

Later, Mr. Guy, who ran the choir for many years, transported us in his converted jeep. On one occasion after **too much** liquid refreshment, Roley White and I became somewhat inebriated much to Mr. Guy's concern!

The Christmas party was a real treat; lots of simple games and party food - rationing was still in force, which made every thing so much more exciting. Mrs Webster would give us a large bag of sweets which was hung on a line across the village hall. Then one of us would be blindfolded, given a stick to unlock it and scatter the sweets for everyone to quickly gather.

In the summer, at odd times, trips to the coast were arranged - another real treat for everybody.

On the way home there would be a sing-song accompanied by comb and paper!

Some of us had jobs in the village. I used to clean the knives and chop the wood for Mrs. Webster. One job I really enjoyed was to wash and clean the Rolls that belonged to Mr. Guy.

Another of my early memories was of a monkey called Jacko which belonged to Mrs. Carter who lived in a cottage at the bottom of Wells Hill. I think she had a relation in the Navy who brought it home. The unfortunate animal was kept in a shed at the back of the house. It wore a little knitted jacket, as I recall, and we children used to often ask if we could see the monkey.

Yet another memory is of German prisoners of war who lived in the timbered cottage at the bottom of Lees Hill. They worked on Frank Butler's farm and the cottage belonged to him. In their spare time they made baskets which I think they sold to the ladies of the village. They made a pigeon basket for my father who used to keep and race pigeons. One Christmas we invited three of them to spend Christmas day with us.

I eventually left South Warnborough to live in Greywell when my father retired. I must say I enjoyed my early years in the village, and even though I was a policeman's son, I was accepted into the adventures and fun of growing up there. I really became a "country boy" and it is sad that the children of today don't have the freedom that we enjoyed!

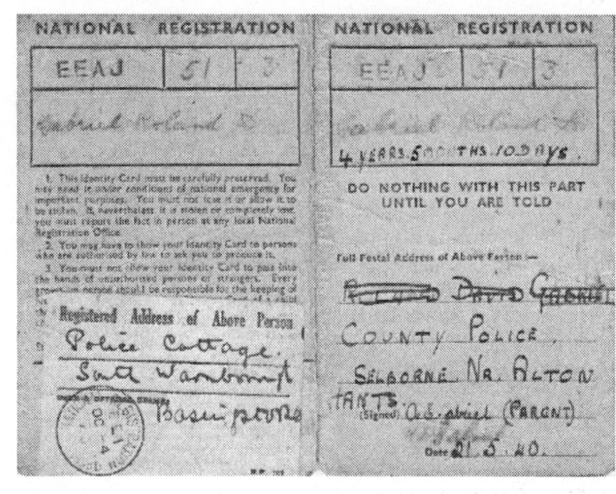
NATIONAL REGISTRATION

| EEAJ | 51 | 3 |
|---|---|---|

Registered Address of Above Person
Police Cottage.
South Warnborough
Basingstoke

NATIONAL REGISTRATION

| EEAJ | 51 | 3 |
|---|---|---|

4 YEARS 5 MONTHS 10 DAYS.

DO NOTHING WITH THIS PART
UNTIL YOU ARE TOLD

Full Postal Address of Above Person :—
COUNTY POLICE.
SELBORNE NR. ALTON
HANTS.
(Signed) (PARENT)
Date 21.5.40.

I started recording my memories by showing my Dad's "police" identity card, so I'm finishing by showing mine – it may be of interest to younger readers?

This photo is to prove we sometimes do have deep snow in Hampshire. It shows my Dad along the Alton road in1951.

A final comment, is that I have noticed the Police House where we lived, is now called "**Roadmans**", whereas the roadman actually lived in the house next door!!

# Joan Goodchild

← My brother Tom, as a young lad.

My brother Tom and I came to the village from Hollybourne when I was four years old and Tom was just a little baby. This was in 1938. Our Dad was a painter and decorator. We had a happy childhood with our Grandparents living close by.

I started at the village school during the war years. It was quite frightening at times with bombs dropping all around us.

As we grew older we had a new addition to the family, Freddie.
We all went to Long Sutton Primary School. The Headmaster was called Mr Willmot who scared us quite a lot, but we got used to it.

When I left school I worked for Mrs Guy, as a nanny to Harriet and Robert.

My friends were Gwen Downs, Marjorie Adlam, Evelyn Smith and many of the other girls in my school.
Here I am with Marjorie in Mrs Papes garden, with the children we looked after.

We attended Sunday school and I joined the choir. The vicar at the time was Rev. Oldfield.

Tom did his City and Guild in painting and decorating, and worked for Goodalls in Basingstoke. Tom played cricket for the village with some of his friends. They were the happy days; we would all go on Sundays to the green to watch them. We would also go to the fetes together.

Tom would enjoy shooting with “General” Woodrow and his son Ray, whenever he could. After the war our Dad worked in London re-building properties that had been destroyed in **The Blitz**. He was also in the Home Guard.

I met my husband in South Warnborough. He was German and had been a prisoner of war. He worked for Mr Butler, the local farmer. We got married at St Andrews Church in 1953 and lived a long and happy life. We had two sons Richard and Stephen who also attended Long Sutton School, as did my grandchildren.

# Tom Goodchild

MY sister Joan helped me with my memories of living in South Warnborough.

We lived at No. 1 Park Cottage, Wells Hill during the war years. I can remember putting up the blackout curtains, the oil lamps flickering and the bombs dropping around us. My mother said that I used to shout “nanny goats” when the doodle bugs came over later in the war.

Mother coped very well on her own, especially as Dad was working in London on bomb damage repair for Milwards of Holybourne. He also did his Home Guard duties in the village.

Dad’s mum lived at Anstey, near Alton, and I used to cycle down Anstey Lane to see her. She used to make homemade apple ginger and gooseberry jams for us. Her landlady, Mrs Hughes looked out for her. Joan and I could never thank her enough for those kind deeds.

Mr and Mrs Roberts

Our granny and granddad lived at New Farm with their son Albert, who worked for Mr Baggs. Albert provided us with lamb’s tails and we would then singe off the wool over candles for mother to make lamb tail pie.

I loved the time I spent with my granddad when he lived at New Farm. We spent time in his copse, cutting bean rods, pea sticks and fire wood. The cart he used was made with pram wheels.

Schooldays

At South Warnborough School, my teacher Mrs Anderson taught Brian Smith, Arthur Knight, Jimmy Spreadborough, Maria Doogan and me.

I always remember the time Arthur tripped up Brian Greenhill in the playground, when waiting to start lessons and Greenhill then crawling into the classroom with a broken leg.

Mrs Anderson later moved into the school house and Brian and I were invited to have tea with her.

Long Sutton School

Mr Wilmot was the headmaster. On one occasion when playing football, I broke a glass and was then told to stand in the corner, where I became a bit fidgety.

I later went to Odiham School.

"General Woodrow and his son Ray

Mr Woodrow was a gamekeeper who lived in the village and often took me rabbiting, using his ferrets. He taught me how to net the burrows and to remain really quiet when rabbiting, as we had to listen very carefully. He also taught me how to run a liner – that is when a rabbit had been killed and the ferret would curl up and not come out. I would put the polecat on a line and let it enter the same hole as the ferret and then chase it out. Ben, the name of the ferret, would never eat the kill, for the very reason that it was always well fed.

Freddie Goodchild

Freddie our brother enjoyed going to school at Long Sutton and later at Odiham. When he was thirteen, he became ill, which started with his left knee swelling. The ambulance took him to Basingstoke Hospital and Mum and Dad followed in the hospital car. Freddie was then taken to Southampton where they found that he had a blood clot. He was immediately rushed to the Atkinson Morley in London. It turned out to be a brain tumour and after the operation it left him paralysed on his left side and partially blind. He had a calliper made for his left leg. Mother cared for him until he passed away.

## Leaving School

When I left school I took up an apprenticeship in painting and decorating with Goodhall Barnard and Clayton of Basingstoke. I spent hours mixing red lead primer using red lead powder.

During my apprenticeship I attended the old Tech College in Worting Road and then went to Winchester Art College to finish my course.

My Firm then built the new Tech. College. I also did a lot of work for Jerimiah Coleman on the Malshanger Estate.

With fellow apprentices, we painted the outside of The Vine, a National Trust house. The lake in the grounds was very pleasant and great to sit by for lunch breaks.

I had a large contract at Smiths Industries, Basingstoke, which meant erecting scaffolding in the workshops to paint the ceilings. We had to cover the machinery between 6 o'clock and twelve midnight to do the work.

In the mornings I enjoyed the toast we had from the canteen.

## My accident

In 1956 I had a motorcycle accident at the bottom of Dean Hill, on my way to work. It was with Parsons fish van from Odiham. Mrs Mosdel, who was our local paper lady, came to my aid.

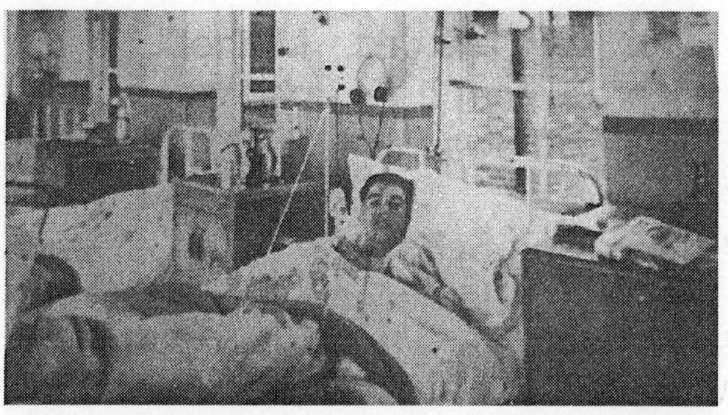

My left leg was on my chest with my foot over my shoulder. I was taken to hospital and was there for 10 months in plaster and on crutches. I was unconscious for three days and I was told that Mr Draper, the village policeman, was there waiting for a statement.

Rudi, my brother-in-law was very angry with me. He was a lovely person and a brilliant table tennis player, who played for the Ridley Hall youth club.

I was eventually transferred to Treloars Hospital, where I had a pin inserted into my femur.

The Plough

The public house was run by Mr and Mrs Trussler. Their son David, Brian Smith and I used to put a tent up in the back garden and have a nice breakfast in the morning. At home we had two lovely cooking apple trees and I used to take some down to Mrs Trussler for her to make apple pies for us.

Albert Simpson was keen on deep-sea fishing and with Tim Casswell, Peter Loader, we fished at Littlehampton, Hayling Island and Mudeford.

My work in the village

I mowed the lawn for Mr and Mrs Guy and worked at the Manor House doing the external painting. My father did the same for Mr Thomas.

I worked on the Bell House for Mr and Mrs Carpenter and did many more jobs at the Manor House.

The Lodge

I used to work for Mrs Nickissons and Mrs Guy at South Warnborough Lodge and over the years I did the internal painting for every room. Also, there were many other jobs I undertook, some of them quite complex.

A crowd of us relax, during a visit to Southend.
My mother is sitting at the table – on the left.

# Harriet Guy

**I** came to SW in 1947 when my grandmother (Mrs Webster) moved her entire family here; she bought The Lodge, which was in a dilapidated state after being commandeered during the war. My unmarried aunt and uncle each had a flat in the house, my aunt and uncle (Nickissons) lived in Stable House and set up riding stables and my parents, recently returned from Nigeria, moved into Upsteps Cottage. It was a new life for everyone.

A family of Polish refugees, (or Displaced Persons as they were then called), also came to live at the Lodge and help my grandmother. The mother, Victoria, was wonderful in the kitchen despite language problems and made me miniature loaves of bread and other treats; Jan kept the garden under control and their daughter Danuta went to school locally. In our attic we still have the handmade wooden trunk that contained all their possessions.

When my brother was only a few months old he was very ill with pneumonia but recovered under the care of Nurse Arnold who visited every day. She was the much-loved and respected District Nurse in the area for a long time. The local doctor that I remember, Dr. Harwood, had his surgery in Odiham but was always prepared to make a home visit and became a family friend. Later on he held a weekly surgery in the kitchen of the Ridley Hall but it was advisable to speak quietly as there were always other patients sitting near the hatch to listen in!

We went to church every week and one of my early memories is of sitting in church next to my grandmother and trying to ignore the fox fur over her shoulder with its menacing eyes and teeth. My father was a churchwarden and got involved with the choir which was then quite sizeable - although that may have had more to do with the annual outings than anything else. I liked helping him to count the collection after the service.

Upsteps Cottage was small but it had a garden large enough to satisfy my father's enthusiasm for gardening and a play area.

There was also room to keep a pig as many families did then.
I remember the day the butcher

came to kill it because of the awful screaming noise – the salted carcase hung in the empty cottage next door all winter and we used to creep in to look at it. The Nickissons kept rabbits instead and, in retrospect, I am not surprised that my cousin Annabel was vegetarian for a long time. Joan Goodchild came to be our Nanny and became an essential part of the family, for several years. Here I am at Upsteps with Joan, my brother Robert and of coarse, Honey the dog.

I caught scarlet fever, measles and the other usual illnesses but the real drama was when I fell out of the car on the way to my dancing class in Alton. My mother, who was driving, didn't notice for a while as she was busy chatting to my friend's mother in the front; finally my friend managed to attract their attention and they went back to pick me out of the ditch and take me home for the gash in my head to be stitched up.

The Freemans ran the shop. It was a fascinating place with enormous glass jars of sweets that you could buy in small quantities to make the coupons go further; my favourite was sherbet lemons. As a gullible child of 9 or 10, I was sent by my Uncle Nick to buy 'striped paint' and a 'left handed paintbrush' from the shop: George Freeman just roared with laughter and made me feel very small.

In the early 50s we moved to the Old Rectory - it was a big house and almost always cold. Robert was keen on WWII and would set out his plastic soldiers and armament, which he marched slowly up the stairs, around the house and down again; the whole manoeuvre could take days and was only complete after many matches had been fired from miniature anti-aircraft guns and enough troops had been knocked down to declare the right side had won, again. I was recruited into moving soldiers and guns but the tactics were always his. Actually, I found my stamp collection more interesting.

We both had bikes from Mr Knight and enjoyed riding along Gaston Lane to the Lookout Tree at the end. We also liked exploring the woods until the day we were chased out by a gamekeeper with a gun, which was rather scary. At home, apart from re-enactments of the Royal Tournament and cowboys and Indians, one of our favourite occupations was to climb along the inside of the big yew hedge from one end to the other, without touching the ground, which could take half a day. While we were living there Joan and Rudi Ceislik got married and I was a bridesmaid. It seemed that almost everyone in the village came to the wedding.

In 1953 South Warnborough celebrated the Coronation with various events including a children's fancy dress parade.

Robert went as Robin Hood, I was dressed as a Kate Greenaway girl and Annabel was a reluctant washerwoman trundling her Triang mangle very slowly and laboriously along the whole route.

At least, we were all given Coronation mugs for taking part although they were broken or lost long ago. The new Queen visited RAF Odiham that year and we all stood in the High Street waving our Union Jacks as she drove by.

Uncle Nick kept a variety of horses and ponies;

He taught me and many other children to ride and we loved exploring the local tracks and woods with him as he was a great naturalist and could recognise every bird by its song; I remember hearing a nightingale near Humbly Grove. He had a tame magpie called Maggie and a pet ferret, which I was rather afraid of.

The Hampshire Hunt sometimes had its meet in the village, either at the bottom of the hill by the Tree and pump or outside the Plough, and my mother

occasionally rode with them.

As a teenager I learnt to make cakes and pastry with Mrs Trussler at the Plough and had driving lessons on the deserted roads at Lasham Airfield with Mr Tyler – one of the kindest men ever. It was very convenient living opposite the Green Garage as he was always willing to help with mechanical repairs even if the problem was only with the lawn mower.

South Warnborough was a good place to grow up. I am glad I still live here and my grandchildren can enjoy it too.

# John Hillyer

Here I am with my mum and brother saying goodbye to my dad as he leaves for work
(June 1935)

However, one of my first memories of life in South Warnborough was the 3rd September 1939. I was just six years old and that Sunday morning I can remember my dad saying that we were at war. It may have seemed frightening but really did not register. But, living through the war time and being an awful thing, it taught me that you can survive on all the natural things such as vegetables from your own garden and eggs from your chickens kept in a natural run in the garden; also wild rabbits.

As time passed I went to the village school and then on to Long Sutton school, being transported by Guy Freeman in his utility vehicle. Sometimes we walked, going through the lanes to make a shortcut and, of course, playing on the way.

Mr Stan Wilmott was our Headmaster and he had the "pleasure" of giving me the cane on my first day. This was for being reported for trying to make a thrush swim in a cattle water trough. I was of course led on by my older friends. Staying on the subject of Stan Wilmott, my Headmaster, I learned more in the school kitchen gardens and woodwork shed than in the classroom. In fact, I did very much better when taking day release at Basingstoke Technical College – I then realised there were fractions and decimals!

Although I did not have a very good education under Mr Wilmott, I learned a lot about life. Most days I had to fill a stone jar with the left over milk for him to take home in his haversack on his motorcycle. I often wondered what happened to all those toys that we made in the woodwork shed. I was very fond of Miss Hoyes, one of our teachers, and I think Stan Wilmott was as well, because he did seem very friendly towards her.

As a young boy we lived a wonderful, natural life. I am now a firm believer in a good immune system.

I can remember eating swedes from the field with much of the dirt still attached to them. The big barn at the start of Lees Hill was where they kept the broken and swept up remains of the biscuits from Huntley & Palmers. I used to open a bag and really go for the pink wafers. This was called cattle cake.

George Spreadborough was my very best friend, and we were quite inseparable, just roaming the countryside and doing a lot of tree climbing. I used to envy Don Silver, my next door neighbour. He could climb higher than anyone else, especially the big ash tree on the boundary of his house. In a way he seemed fearless. Surprisingly, not one of us ever seemed to come a cropper and if we did, it was never serious.

Roy Oliver, being the same age as me, was also very active in village life and he always seemed to be up to something or other!

The village toffs as I called them, were very nice people. The Pilkingtons (from the glass Company) lived in the Manor House and arranged a fete during the summer. This was a good and very much a looked for occasion.

The sister of Mr Pilkington (Miss Pilkington) lived in Vine Cottage, Lees Hill. I had the great pleasure of working for her from the age of 11 until 14. I walked across two fields every morning, creating a footpath, to fill two scuttles with coke for her boiler, and to feed the chickens. This I did again at the finish of school. I received the wonderful sum of 10 shillings a week. My dad was only on three pounds for a full week. She treated me very well indeed.

I think South Warnborough was unique inasmuch as there were two garages, two shops, a pub, a village hall and a church - wonderful.

In our village of there was no vandalism or theft, and we had a high respect for our elders. My mum and dad were absolutely wonderful parents to my brother Ray, our sister Ann and me. It was all about nature and respect. When my friends in the village had broken bicycles they used to say "take it up to Uncle George" (that was my dad) "and he will fix it."

I can remember going out with George Spreadborough, Roy Oliver, Roland White and others early on a Saturday morning, returning just before dark, surviving on what you could find. Mum and dad seemed not to have worried that we were away all that time.

We had two air raid shelters at our school. They were covered in a very thick layer of earth. I remember the rabbits used to burrow in the earth and Stan Wilmott would net the holes and fix a flexible tube to the exhaust from his motorbike into one of the holes, to force them to run out into the net (they would probably be his dinners).

The village church played quite a role in our lives. Singing in the choir every Sunday morning and evening. We had a wonderful rector called Reverend Oldfield. After evensong on Sunday evening, he would call in at the local pub called The Plough, where the landlord was Mr Trussler. He would drink a pint with the locals and always had a packet of twenty Players. You may wonder how I knew what went on in the pub at my young age - I used to peep through the window!

I mowed the vast lawns for Reverend Oldfield. My wage would be sixpence. I think I would have done it for nothing for being allowed, at my young age, to use his Atco Motor Mower with a kick-start.

I can remember during the war when they built the runways at Lasham Airfield. There seemed to be a continuous convoy of lorries, belonging to Ham River, passing through the village and carrying aggregates for the construction work.

Another recollection of village life was every Wednesday they held a Whist Drive in the village hall. They were very pleasant evenings. Probably I was 14 before I was allowed to play.

There was another great character from Humbly Grove Farm. He was called Jack Simpson (or Captain John Simpson), the son of Mr and Mrs Simpson who were gentlemen farmers. Jack Simpson was eccentric and always followed the hounds in red regalia. Every Sunday he walked from Humbly Grove to the church, probably two and a half miles, strutting along with swinging walking stick. My parents later told me that when passing our home, I would strut behind him imitating his walking manner, complete with swinging stick, much to the amusement of our neighbours. Later on in the fifties, he moved to Fleet, taking with him one of the tractors, then once a week my father who worked as a mechanic for Chapels in Odiham, had to go and start up the Fordson Tractor and leave it running while they enjoyed a gin and tonic. That's what you call eccentricity, but he gave a sparkle to our village life.

On leaving school in 1947 work was not easy to come by, and Mrs Webster from Highgate in London bought South Warnborough Lodge and with her came the building firm of J L Collins from her home area. So I went to the lodge to see the foreman and asked if he had a job for me. His reply was "You're not very big, but we'll give you a try" so I started as a dogsbody. They came down by truck from London every Monday morning and went back Friday afternoon. They lived in the hayloft above the stables. Every morning I had to go at 7.00 am and make tea and give it to them in bed. At midday they would go to the pub, probably for two hours, come back and do three or four hours work before going to the pub for the evening. No wonder Mr Collins eventually went bust. Mrs Webster was a very nice person and treated everybody well.

South Warnborough had a cricket team and played surrounding villages on Sunday afternoons. It was really quite an event, especially when I was allowed to hang the figures on the scoreboard. I remember one man in particular called Feller Silver (funny name). He had part of his arm amputated, I think maybe due to a shotgun accident, but he overcame this with a ring fixed to the end and he was probably one of the best batsmen in the team. For a living he was a professional rabbit catcher, going out with his ferrets all day and returning with a rod on his shoulder, with probably twenty rabbits already paunched and ready for skinning. He sold them to the locals and butchers.

During the years between 1930 and 1950 it was customary on a Sunday afternoon for your parents to invite their friends for Sunday tea, and we played cards and board games which was jolly good fun. One thing that sticks in my mind was

Phyllis Stent saying to my mother, Margaret, "When are you going to let John wear long trousers?" I was nearly fourteen! I can remember often looking at my legs in the winter and they were bright red. I am now 75 years old and still suffer no knee problems (it makes you think).

One thing that I am not very proud about, (but you were at the time! -- brother), is in April 1953 I was outside the village hall while a whist drive was in progress. Egged on by my friends, they opened the doors, and I rode my motorcycle in between the tables. I must have been reported to PC Gabriel. He came to my house the next day, but I had just left to start my National Service! This was also a very important time in my life, ending up in Cyrenacia (now Libya), the only time I have been abroad or been in an aircraft.

Two photos

– Here am I me, looking smart! >

Just before I left the Army, I had my photo taken with my brother Ray, who had enlisted in the RAF on a short-term engagement.

Whilst at Long Sutton School I used to sit next to Daphne Knight. She was a clever girl and used to quite often come to the top of the class in our exams. I remember often trying to glance at her papers to get the right answers! Also, I can remember asking her to be my sweetheart. She agreed. I cannot remember how long it lasted.

Simple things seemed to give so much pleasure. There were cottages at the corner of Wells Hill and Alton Road. When it was dark we used to fix a cord onto the door knocker and take it across the road and pull it, and delight in seeing the occupant open the door and no-one being there! Ha Ha!

During the war, the men that were not in the services for being exempt for various reasons joined the LDV (Local Defence Volunteers) later to become the Home Guard (more like Dads' Army)! On Sundays in the village they used to parade and march up and down the road. At 12.00 they ended up at the pub!

My mother later told me that on one occasion my dad, after being on look-out at Wells Hill during the expected invasion from Germany, came home and later said "I have left my ammunition at my out-post", so he went back to recover it but it was not there. Later my mother found it in the cupboard so he had not even taken it with him!

Mr Stent was the shepherd for Mr Butler's Farm spending most of his time fixing hurdles into pens for the sheep. He did this through all the rain and the snow as just a matter of course.

Harvest time was a great time for me as I used to lead the horses and carts to collect the sheaves to form a rick, later to be thrashed for corn. At lunchtime we sat at the hedgerow. I remember Mr Spreadborough had a bottle of homemade beer. It was dark in colour and made by his wife. I also remember having a sip or two and really liking it! We used to line up on Friday evenings to be paid by Frank Butler. This was fourpence per hour in old money.

Leading on from the Manor House was an avenue of Lime trees. Dozens of Jackdaws used to build their nests in the bushy part of the trees. We used to collect the eggs. Further up was the rookery where at a certain time they would shoot at the rooks and these were used to make rook pie (Yuk)!

Westers Lane was a popular walk, especially during the summer. One of the most popular birds to be seen was the Yellowhammer, building a rather scruffy nest and laying eggs of off-white with dark scribbling lines. Today it is still my favourite bird.

A school photo >>>

I can remember the three-cornered meadow where a family lived in a caravan and tent, working for the Butlers (the farmers) mainly, hoeing out weeds between various crops; they used to cook their food on open fires. One of the girls came to our school and always seemed to smell of bonfires!

During the war the Army used to camp in the field opposite our house. My friends and my brother Ray used to go out and talk to them and would often enjoy some of their food. My favourite was cake and custard eaten from a mess tin. They treated us very well and gave us such things as regimental overcoat buttons and cap badges which were proudly displayed on our belts. Also there were the Canadian soldiers who camped between South Warnborough and Long Sutton. They used to give us food cooked over a tin filled with sand and oil. They smoked Sweet Caporal cigarettes with three dimensional pictures of aircraft on the back of the packet. I did collect the complete set.

Throughout my account of my life in South Warnborough I go from one thing to another, never in order, but that was how life was then, nothing in a set order so now on to some more memories.

One of the most interesting activities was birds' nesting. We used to spend hours on end just looking for birds' nests and forming a collection of eggs, only ever taking one when there were several in the nest, or if only one or two, going back a few days later to take one for my collection. I can remember finding a whitethroat's nest in the bank at Wells Hill. This was a very difficult nest to find. I eventually took one egg for my collection.

I can remember going to South Warnborough Youth Club. We played table tennis and darts amongst other things, and it was always very enjoyable. I walked home in the dark and sometimes thought it was very scary and would start to run, but there was no need because there were never any dangers or problems.

Owen Tyler, who kept the green garage, being a very keen motorcyclist, would invite the boys of the village to go to his house of an evening and watch picture slides of the various motorcycle races. We thought this was great fun. No wonder with his enthusiasm, he was still riding his vintage motorcycle into his nineties.

Brian Butler the son of the farmer Frank Butler was a very good horseman and excelled in jumping competitions. His fame was winning the Horse of the Year Show on a horse called Tankard. It made the villagers very proud of him.

After the war I remember, probably for the first time, having bananas and ice cream as a very special treat, maybe on a Sunday, or if my parents could afford it. Luxuries such as this were very rare and very much looked forward to. For several years this was normal and you expected nothing else. This gave you a very good standing in life.

Another occasion was at Christmas when we would gather together to go carol singing at Powntley Copse to sing at the toffs' houses. We would enjoy a mince pie and a glass of juice and collect a small donation for the Church. It was probably a three mile round trip, but great fun.

Although now the village consists mainly of newcomers, from what I can gather there still seems to be a good village spirit, with the Church and shop being central points, and I often have chats with Gale, who is a customer of mine, and she talks very enthusiastically about the village. This is a very good sign indeed. I hope it may well continue as this is very essential for a good village community.

I have tried to keep my memories alive by taking my son, Andrew, to all the haunts of my early life in the village, such as the Avenue, The Rookery, Westers Lane and The Mill at Greywell. He is now following my footsteps by going there with his girlfriend, Sarah. They very much enjoy it, because things there are still so natural.

Also, Mrs Webster's two daughters came to live in the village; Mrs Nichisson and Mrs Guy. They blended in with the village very well. Mr Nickisson was a good horseman and made great use of the existing stables. I remember Mr Nickisson asking me if I would dig a series of post holes to form a paddock. He said he would pay me sixpence for each hole dug. I thought this would be very good, not realising it was solid chalk and flint! I probably managed one hole an evening.

Threshing time was also great fun. There would be a threshing machine driven by a large belt run by a fly wheel on a Fordson tractor. The sheaves of wheat, barley or oats were pitched into the drum of the machine. The corn would go from a chute to fill big sacks and the straw and chaff would come out the other side. We, as children, would stand close to and try to kill the rats and mice that ran out.

Our milk each day was delivered to our house by Mrs Webb from Dean Farm, originally from a churn, and ladled into a waiting jug. Later on it was delivered in milk bottles with a waxed cardboard top pressed into the neck of the bottle. This had a centrepiece that you pressed in to pull out the top. I remember she used to make her deliveries in an old car with the top cut off.

During the early part of the war we had no electricity. Lighting was by way of oil lamp and the wireless was powered by an accumulator. This was a glass type container filled with an acid with two terminals to connect to the wireless. From time to time we had to take it to Mr Tyler's garage to be recharged. This was sixpence a time. Later on we had electricity. One exciting thing about this was on Sunday evenings we, as a family, played cards – Snap, Rummy and Beat Jack Neighbour Out of Doors. My dad, for a special treat, would say "John, get your torch out" (which was probably my main Christmas present) "and shine it at the light". He would take out the 40 watt bulb and replace it with a 60 watt to give a stronger light for a special treat. After the card evening was over he repeated this, by taking out the 60 watt bulb and replacing it with the 40 watt, until the next Sunday. That's what you call thrift (every penny counted).

I can remember my mother telling me that when my brother Ray started school, that on his first day, she had to drag him bawling all the way. He was a very positive kid, and used to have quite a temper. I remember him being told off one day, and he struck out at the sitting room door with his foot, and broke the panelling. I have to say this is probably the only time I have got one over on him, as the reason he got his telling off was because I had been annoying him and he'd retaliated. While we were out playing he would be indoors studying. No wonder he was later to become an egg-head. He certainly made it in a big way.

Here we are as youngsters – I'm not sure of the year.

As I am writing this, I am within a few days of celebrating 50 years of running my own business of plumbing and heating. My son Andrew is now a partner in the business. If I had my time over again I would not dream of changing it. Hopefully, I still have a few more years to go!

How times have changed. In the centre of the village we had a pond. In the winter it used to freeze over, and whilst waiting for our school taxi, we would run and slide over the ice. You could hear it cracking under our weight, but it was great fun.

Going back to South Warnborough Lodge, I have to say that an ex German Prisoner of War named Martin built a wall approximately 100 yards long, from the Lodge going down hill to the cottages. He built it sloping inwards and gave it a mottled finish by throwing cement mixture through a metal sieve. This gave it a very good finish. This was the only time that I have ever seen this happen. He was a very nice person and very hard working, and the wall is still there today.

The first house past the Village Hall going up Lees Hill was called Manor Court. It was unfinished with a glass dome on the roof, all the window spaces were boarded up, and inside was very dark. As kids, we played in this building. It was always very scary. There were no stairs, but somehow we managed to get onto the first floor. The house stayed in this state for many years. Maybe the builder went bust, but who knows. Today it is all finished and quite elegant.

At the Lodge they had a gardener named Tom Cripps. He always seemed to be working very hard and kept the gardens in good condition. There was a greenhouse, like a lean-to, on a high brick wall. In it were vines.

I can remember another weekly occasion when we had our shopping delivered by a Mr Emerson. He worked for International Stores. He brought the groceries from a list that my mother had given him the week before. He used to tick the items off and my mother would pay him, and give him the list for the next week. He then used to sit down and have a cup of tea with us. He was a jolly man and used to make us laugh.

My mother used to get her day to day shopping at the village shop.

South Warnborough is situated between three towns – Basingstoke, Alton and Odiham. When we could afford it we used to go by bus to Basingstoke on a Saturday afternoon and go to the cinema. We had a choice of three – The Odeon, The Waldorf, and The Plaza or "The Fleapit". We also rode our bikes to Alton and to The Palace Cinema. My favourite film star was Roy Rogers and his horse Trigger. We used to stand and cheer when he pulled off one of his amazing stunts. Before riding back home we would go to Mr Campbell's and have fish and chips which were wrapped in newspaper. We used to just leave our bikes wherever, but they were always there when we returned. Often we would go to Odiham Cinema at the weekend. I remember one occasion while we were cycling home and it was very dark, and Morris Ash who was with us, but was much older, saw in the distance two small lights coming towards us. Thinking it was a pair of cyclists he said "I am going to turn off my light and give them a scare by riding in between them". Much to his surprise it was a stationary car with small parking lights, one on each wing. I think he had to carry his bike home!

I remember during this period I felt very good to have a navy blue overcoat and a long white scarf. This was the ultimate! I suppose this was the prelude to becoming a Teddy Boy.

Another time of my life in the village was to go and work, at the age of fourteen, for Mr Merton in Greywell. He ran a plumbing business. He was a very good plumber and in actual fact they called him "The Midnight Plumber" because he talked all day and worked all night. I think some of this has rubbed off on me. My parents used to get upset when I arrived home on my bicycle at 8.00 or 9.00 o'clock at night for my dinner. They used to moan like billy-o. He carried out his business on a motorcycle and box side car. His fame was to ride from South Warnborough cross roads to Long Sutton cross roads with the side car wheel off the road (how mad)! Although he was a good plumber, I remember on one occasion when at the end of the day we tested the system that we had been working on, and behold the basin had two cold water connections, and the WC had hot water as a result of always talking! He also smoked cigarettes called Turf. He used to hold these between his teeth and they used to become very soggy and didn't last very long! One day we were working on repairs to a lead flat roof. It was very cold and he said to me "I'm just going down for a while". I waited and was freezing, so I lay on my tummy and looked through the bathroom window below, and saw him kissing the Swiss maid! He eventually rejoined me to carry on working!.

I will now mention my sister Ann. She was several years younger than me and seven years younger than Ray, that's why we never played together very much (I wasn't into dolls, anyway)! She was a very pretty girl with auburn hair and had friends of her own age. Being the only girl and the youngest of the family, my dad doted on her. I think she was a bit spoilt, but she did well at school and always had a job. She later married and had a son and daughter, and I still go to see her quite regularly.

Having now related the sunny side of my life in the village I will now go a little into the darker side. As previously mentioned I worked as a lad for the wonderful Miss Pilkington. I was probably about twelve years old, and one morning going there to do my chores getting in the coal, etc, I walked into the carriage garage to fill the scuttles and in front of me was a fire ablaze. I panicked and raced back to the house, and shouted up the stairs to Miss Pilkington "The garage is on fire!" She called the fire brigade and I raced round to the farm next door and told the farm workers what had happened. They came round and wheeled the Rover car outside and put out the remains. It had nearly burnt to the ground.

That morning the Police came to the school to interview me. As you can probably imagine, nothing much happens in a village, but when it does, the gossip really gets going. Such that probably I had been smoking (which was not true, and Miss Pilkington knew this). Fortunately, Mrs Webb, the milk lady, said she had seem smoke coming from the property long before I had arrived, and thought it was from an overnight bonfire, so there was my alibi. According to the insurance company, it turned out to have been caused by a blow-out from the coal! To this day the floor of the building is still there and has never been rebuilt.

The other black day was in early 1954 when my father, George, was attending to a difficult tractor tyre at Chapels where he worked as a tractor mechanic, and it blew up, with the wheel taking an inch off his lower lip and damaging his nose, and it then went through the roof of the garage. He went to Rooksdown Hospital for plastic surgery, but after quite a short period of time, he was the usual happy George Hillyer.

I have got to stop now as it will go on forever. It was like living in a dream world, and I have relayed these stories to you to the best of my memory.

To say what my life in South Warnborough meant to me is summed up by the following: Now as we drive past Odiham Aerodrome and to the hill leading to Long Sutton crossroads, looking out at the wonderful view of the village and surroundings, I say out aloud

**"My beloved South Warnborough."**

# Ray Hillyer

## My Early Years and Memories

This is the earliest photograph I have, showing me at nine months, with my Mum and Dad, outside of the cottage where I was born. This **memorable** occasion was on the 25th October 1930.

Well! Here I am, looking very angelic at thirteen months.

Walter George and Margaret Nellie (George & Nell) moved into No2 Park Cottages, South Warnborough that year from Droxford where they had been living with Dad's mum (Nanny Hillyer-senior) for a few weeks.

We lived next door to the Amer family who became good friends of ours. Ray Amer was slightly older than me and his sister, Jean, was about my age. This brings me to the first part of my theory on early memories - frights! (excitements, being the other)

There was a high bank at the end of our house and Ray Amer decided we should take it in turns to jump off the bank on to the path below, by the end of the house. The game was OK until I hit the wall head first! Did I scream? - I do wonder whether the bump still affects me? I guess I was about three years old at the time.

The second fright occurred at the end of one of our, what was to be, regular Sunday walks. I was pushing my brother in the pram, when I stumbled and let the pram go! I started yelling, then like a greyhound Dad raced by and managed to grab the pram just as it accelerated down the hill and into possible trouble!

I have no more memories or photographs associated with Wells Hill. The very next time I remember, is when we moved into No 2 Council Houses, Alton Road. I was probably about four years old.

I can recall Bob Spreadborough driving a four wheeled horse and wagon, piled up with our furniture, together with the rest of our few belongings, pulling up outside our new home.

What **scared** me, were five Silver children, all bigger than me, leaning over the fence, staring and laughing! I realised a long time afterwards it was a perfectly natural thing to do, (i.e. in the thirties, you made your own fun!), but it's still remembered as a fright!

Mum, John and a little giggling me, seeing Dad off to work at Chapples, a Fordson tractor dealer in Odiham.

Enjoying Sunday on the lawn, (The village football and cricket pitch in the field opposite).

Ray, on his way to becoming a first class cricketer, No wonder I didn't make it, I'm naturally left handed!!

One of the strongest memories from my childhood is that after a hard week at work, Dad would always find the time to take us for a walk in the country. His overall knowledge of the wildlife in the South of England was outstanding. Whether it was birds, animals, flowers, grasses or any other aspect of the countryside, he could guide us and explain in such a friendly way that we've remembered those walks to this day.

I don't know if it's in our genes or outright enthusiasm - could be a combination of both? It has remained one of my main interests throughout the whole of my life, and still is, I'm pleased to say!

I followed in Dad's footsteps and imparted the enthusiasm and hopefully, some knowledge to both of our children, who in turn are doing the same to their children - what a terrific heritage!

## Primary School

The next step was starting school in the village. We lived in a semi-detached house, with Mrs

Bowie, the headmistress and only teacher, living next door – another frightening experience!

During the 1930's, it was normal practice for senior employees of Hampshire County Council to be assigned a council house.

When the great day came for me to go off to school for the first time, I would not go! - I screamed and wrapped myself around a chair and Mum could not break me free! So the next day, Mum persuaded Mrs Bowie to help. I was dragged down the road, past Bob Spreadborough, who was digging potatoes with a horse drawn spinner in the adjacent field. I can still remember him laughing at my efforts to not go to school.

Eventually, after a few mornings of **crying** for my Mum! I settled down to enjoy school very much. What can I remember of those days? – Unfortunately, only a few events.

* The school had the traditional iron railings with spikes on top to keep children inside the playground. During one playtime, a senior girl was leaning over the railings. She slipped and a spike went into her armpit! How she got to hospital, I do not know? (The above photograph, taken in 2007 shows the railings, but not the cross rails)

* The local Council were resurfacing a nearby road, and at lunch-time, completely against the rules to leave the playground, Don Silver and I

went down to watch. We stayed watching, way past the ringing of the school bell signifying the start of school lessons. Then a very angry headmistress suddenly grabbed us by the arm and dragged two shaking boys back to the classroom for our punishment!

* The school was directly in line with the main runway at RAF Odiham, which meant we could

watch the aircraft as they took off and flew over the village. On an afternoon playtime, three Hawker Hectors flew over and were gradually disappearing, when they collided and we could see the aircrew falling out of the aircraft. Some parachutes opened, but others didn't!

The aircraft shown is from No.13 Squadron, Odiham.

Life has some very strange co-incidences! - nearly thirty years later, I was looking after a project for Kelvin & Hughes, which entailed visiting a Company in Bracknell to monitor some sub-contract design work. Over lunch, the draughtsman was talking about his experiences in his earlier career at RAF Odiham. It happened that the three aircraft mentioned were in his flight and he related the incident from his point of view - rather grisly!

- The last and the funniest, was when one boy jumped into the walled ditch on the upper side of the classroom. His aim was to catch a frog, which he did, but then he couldn't get out of the ditch. Instead of helping our classmate, we just stood back and laughed at his predicament!

So, remembering the frights with an occasional funny!

The war (WW2) started during my time at South Warnborough School. My experiences of the war, including those whilst at school, together with the remainder of my later times in the village, are covered later.

## Home Life

I can remember my early years as being very happy and I enjoyed playing with my brother John.

Dad always spent time with us at weekends, either going for nature walks or playing games. He also helped me to master riding a small tricycle and later on, a two-wheeler.

Then came the time when we all joined gangs, and that meant **only** mixing with boys of our own age - i.e. no younger brothers or girls in tow!

It was also a thrill to catch the Ruby Queen bus into Alton - six miles away - often to go to the cinema. Occasionally, on a Sunday, all the family would catch a train from Alton to Droxford, where Dad's parents lived.

Quite often it was a "big gathering" of numerous cousins, aunts and uncles and it was always plenty of fun. At meal times all the children ate meals at a separate table hidden from the adults by a heavy curtain. Play-time was full of chasing and shouting! When we were the only family at Droxford, we would spend a lot of time down at the river Meon which meandered through the meadows behind the church. Tiddler catching was a must! Dad bought the small nets from a nearby shop, which still exists - but probably not selling fishing nets?

We also learnt to "swim" in the river, even though the water did not come over our bodies, when we were stretched out and resting on the gravel bottom!

Our sister Ann, born in 1937, is with Dad and we are in the **deepest** part of the river, away from our swimming area! At this stage, and as I was nearly seven years older I cannot remember very much about the baby in the family.

Here is Mum with the "baby" sitting on the bridge over the **mighty** river – I'm in the background.

## Senior School

When we became eight years old we transferred to Long Sutton School, which was about two miles away.

We travelled in Guy Freeman's shooting brake, which was adapted to take a host of children, all pushed in, with the older ones getting the best seats! (my turn would eventually come!) He went out to Swaine's Hill to pick up a few children before collecting us at the "Cross Tree".

Above, is a rather sombre photograph of my new school, which outwardly, has changed little to this day. Then it had three classrooms, with just one teacher in each and responsible for three classes. The infant classroom is on the left and the senior on the right.

Reflecting on my time there, it was generally a very good school life, but the school was sadly lacking in any academic aims, with little drive at all. Absolutely no activities were available after school - the headmaster, Stan Wilmot, disappeared on his motorcycle within minutes of the final bell! A senior boy always free-wheeled his bike from the garage where it was kept, down to the school gate ready for his quick departure home! I eventually had my turn with the bike!

It was very much to my later disgust, that there was no enthusiasm for the eleven plus, or consultation with parents about the opportunity. In my time at the school I can't remember any pupil going forward for the exam. Some of my contemporaries, where parents paid the fees, would leave to go to either Odiham or Eggars Grammar Schools.

Later I was to make up lost ground the hard way, part-time, and over many years of study. (Eventually, I went to both Southampton and Cardiff Universities, the latter by courtesy of the Royal Air Force).

Wednesday sports afternoon was always good fun, with regular cricket and football matches. When the days were very hot we went to a swimming pool in a large garden in Long Sutton, where the water always seemed to be of a deep green, due to large sycamore trees hanging over the pool. We also used it some evenings and occasionally on Saturdays, having to walk the two miles to and from home. The pool was only refilled about once a season and it took ages before the water felt warm enough to be really enjoyable. I can't remember any boy becoming ill from swallowing this horrible green liquid, particularly the new comers who had to go through a ritual of being held by their hands and feet and thrown in several times – swimmers or not

**Life around the Village**

The "Cross Tree" was special, inasmuch that it was the centre of the village and always used as the "gang's" meeting place. There was a seat around the tree and many of the locals would meet there in the evenings for a chat and a smoke! The tree was also the bus stop for the buses to Alton and Basingstoke.

Above all, it was a huge hollow elm tree, with not only a hole at ground level, but others at higher levels - lending itself as a super fun place. Later in my boyhood our gang hammered spikes on the inside (acquired from a military source!), making it easier to reach the higher holes. Much later, the lower hole was filled with concrete - early "health and safety"! Unfortunately, the tree caught Dutch elm disease and was eventually replaced with a new sapling, now well established.

**S**pecific memories include,

Meeting the ice cream salesman, who had cycled into the village on a tricycle - one wheel at the back with a large freezer box at the front of his machine. He sold small round ice creams, Lyons, I believe, at 2d each. Where he came from, I do not know - probably from Odiham - but during the summer he turned up on the same day every week!

As we became older, occasionally our Sunday walks, took us as far afield as either the White Horse pub known as "Bumpers" (no longer a pub) or the Golden Pot. These were special treats as it was always lemonade and crisps - with the little blue coloured paper twist of salt inside.

Another special occasion, just before the war, was visiting RAF Odiham on Air Display Days. I remember the aerobatics by a flight of Hawker bi - planes, followed by the aircraft flying in to "bomb a castle" with bags of flour. I believe this started my life-time interest in aircraft and eventually into a career within the aerospace industry!!

The village had two shops, a small one attached to the garage (next to the Plough Inn), which no longer exists and the main one opposite the church. In recent years it was helped to remain open by members of the village. I believe it is now privately owned.

This photo was taken in 1997 and the only difference from the thirties is the removal of the wall and the making of a lay-by. Otherwise the front of the shop still looked the same!

The shop had a large bakery at the rear which looked after the bread requirements for the whole village. Obviously, there was no self-service - you just waited your turn.

I can remember there was only one type of cheese, a large cylindrical lump of the Cheddar type. When required, the grocer used a thin wire to cut off a wedge! The photo below, is of a typical shop lay-out of that time.

An experience to do with shopping in the village - on one occasion I was sent to shop for Mum, using her "sit up and beg" bike. I absent-mindedly walked home and many hours later I was sent back to the village to look for it and to find it still leaning against the shop wall!

On a Saturday, the International Stores or Gilbert Dicker for groceries and Robert Mayes or Monks for meat served the village. The order for the following week would be placed at the same time.

As a fairly independent young boy in the village, I would wander, either on my own or with some of the gang over the whole area, such that we new every hedgerow, copse and **unoccupied house**! We also knew where to go and when to go! We were never home unless the weather was extremely wet or we were famished!

One property, which in a way became our favourite, was the very large house next to the village hall. It was basically, a shell, several storeys high, with a big dome on top.
The house was the gang's delight, particularly in creating ways of reaching the very top! Don't mention this to our beloved "Health and Safety"! Wildlife included barn owls, bats, jackdaws and dozens of house sparrows and starlings. Above all, we were soon able to always outwit the caretaker, even when he came round at dusk with his torch. He thought he knew who the intruders were? but we were never caught, therefore no proof?

Our policeman - I've just remembered his name - P.C. Chapman, well! he had other, much easier crimes to resolve?

I was, (for a period of about two days - my words) banned by my father for any involvement in gang activities. The reason was that the gang leader had been caught breaking into a locked shed - one of P.C. Chapman's rare successes!

See page 116 for information on our gang leader.
- Odiham Magistrates Court and a fine of five shillings!

I had quite a few hobbies, mainly collecting items of keen interest, with a few falling by the wayside, such as stamps.

**B**ird's eggs This was a very popular hobby, but became illegal many years ago. Dad laid down a strict rule that one egg only was taken and then when there was more than one in the nest. The bird was then unlikely to desert the nest, but would replenish her clutch of eggs.

**C**igarette cards

Most of the lads collected, because smoking was widespread in the1930/40s and all cigarette packets had a card inside. Swopping was a daily activity, particularly if there was a topical series in print with a military content! Tobacconists sold the albums for holding the cards.

**M**ilitary cap badges

We copied this hobby from the servicemen, who in WW2, fixed badges to their waist belts. It was quickly picked up by the boys and became yet another swopping hobby!

(I have continued to collect to this day, helped a lot by my extensive travels and working with various Air Forces and Military establishments).

## The Choir

I did join for a little while, but it certainly was not for my singing ability - which is about two on a scale of 1 to 10! – it was for the money at 1d / attendance!!

This old photo is of the church and two of the cottages which housed employees of the Manor,

one of them being the head gardener - who we new **well** from our fruit scrumping! The photo was probably taken in the 1930s, as the fencing and the gates disappeared during WW2. I was baptised and confirmed in the church, and went to Sunday school in the village hall. The majority of my contemporaries also attended until **we** all became "too old".

**S**port

It was either football or cricket played in the field opposite where I lived, which was very convenient, such that I didn't miss many kick-abouts. I just didn't take to cricket very much, so concentrated on football. I am naturally left footed, which meant I had less rivalry for the outside left position, especially as I was also a fast runner. I played Basingstoke local league football until I was 37 – when my speed had gone!

It was always the custom to go outside immediately after breakfast and to stay out until I was very hungry. When I joined the gang we were quite often gone for the day, maybe with a hunk of bread in my pocket to keep me going! We would go for miles and just have lots of fun and many times "get into mischief" - whatever that means!

Scrumping was a must when in season and many times took place right under the nose of the owner or head gardener. We quickly learnt to melt into the background. Also, sliding down hayricks time after time and always outrunning the angry farmer, when **spotted!**

So is the photo below a mug shot of a criminal and would a jury find this innocent looking young lad guilty of assisting in the crimes of the village? I don't know the date of this photo, but it was certainly taken at one of the schools?

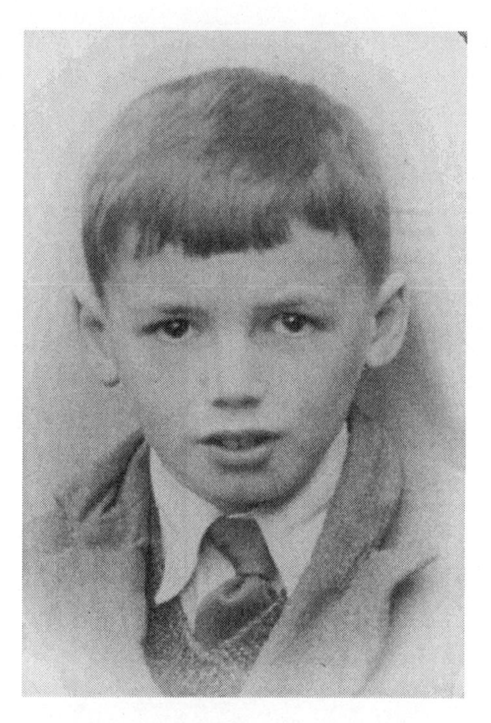

Very few photographs were taken or allowed during my schooldays - due to lack of money and later very strict wartime restrictions - but here are two of the **whole** school, one taken in 1937 (our front cover and included by other contributors).

As you can tell from her appearance, Mrs Bowie ruled with a firm hand - probably necessary? I'm the one wearing a cap.

My brother is sitting in the front row of this photo. (3rd from Rt.) His best friend, George, is in the centre.

Always two pranksters!

In the background is the police house!

The gang graduated to catapults, with the best forks - U-shaped - being those cut from a privet hedge. Of course that meant secretly cutting into someone's well cultivated hedge - so was that an offence?

Our village policeman lived on the corner of Gastons Lane - see above! - It was inevitable that we would eventually be "nabbed" by P.C. Chapman. So when it happened our catapults were confiscated. Our next move was to (mildly?) threaten his son to get hold of our weapons from his father's office. I can't remember the nature of the threat but I do know we also gave him some cherished sweets as a mild form of bribery to keep quiet! We got our catapults back!!

We became accurate shooters, with rabbits and squirrels being our main live targets. I still have the same catapult, albeit a few changes of elastic over the years, before being discarded into the "might come in handy" box in my workshop. We later graduated to air guns, always hidden down our trouser leg when going through the village.

As I reflect more and more experiences come tumbling back, but I need to draw a line somewhere? However, there will be others associated with my time in the village during WW2?

I just had to mention our gang leader, Owen Smith, a good friend and someone I've always admired.

Owen was the son of the roadman living next door to Roland Gabriel, one of our Contributors.

Owen enlisted into the Royal Hampshire Regt. and was sent to South Korea in the early 50's. His Regt. was then attached to the Gloucestershire Regt. The Glosters were at the forefront of the battle of Imjin River when they were overrun by a horde of Chinese infantry, who were assisting the North Koreans.
In the ensuing battle, many of Owen's friends and fellow soldiers were either killed or taken prisoner. Owen crawled under some of the bodies and feigned death as the Chinese bayoneted anyone showing signs of life. He stayed there until nightfall, when he, over several nights, made his way back to Allied lines.

Owen said his survival was helped, not only with his military training, but also with his earlier experiences of growing up as a young lad in South Warnborough and the surrounding countryside.

Unfortunately, Owen is not able to contribute to our book.

## Ray's Wartime

"The day war broke out" is a well known catch-phrase from a comedian of those times - Robb Wilton. It is very much implanted in my mind!

It was just after 11a.m., when Dad, who had been listening to the "wireless", came out into the garden to speak to us. As we all sat on the grass in the sunshine, he told us that England was at war with Germany. What did this mean to a young lad of nearly nine? Very much a mixture of excitement and fear!

The excitement came from watching soldiers at camp in Droxford, during a recent visit to my grandparents. On the downs nearby, were soldiers camped and teams of horses pulling field guns. Was this the way another war would be fought?

- Little did I know!

After all, it was a just a short time from WW1 and the acute economic depression that followed - at that time I knew nothing, or very little about those hard times! Much later, it became obvious to me, for why our military was so out-dated.

The fear came from the unknown, which was to change dramatically in the years to come. For the first time, I started to take an interest in the Daily Mail newspaper delivered every morning. On the front page there was always map or maps showing the latest war situation, which continued throughout the war. It was also an excellent insight into world geography.

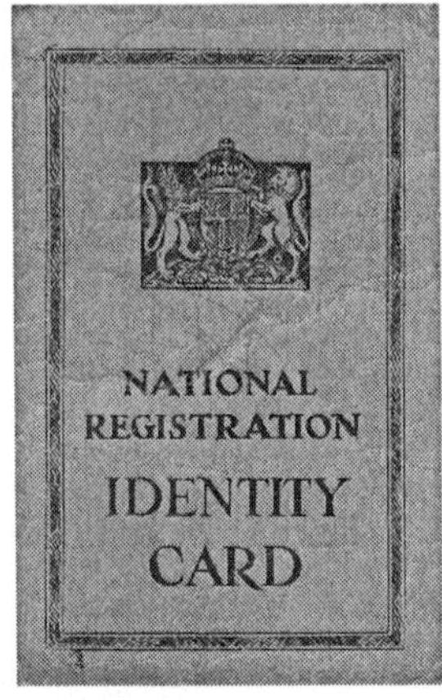


Within months, the German army were approaching the English Channel? So what can I remember next? - The issuing of identity cards. I can still

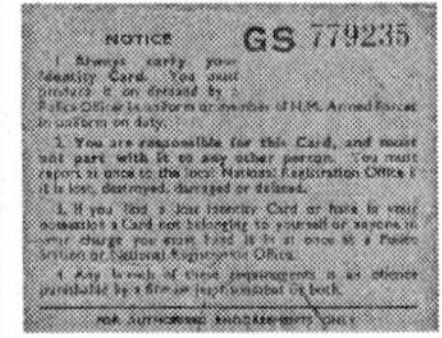


remember my number - EEIE/11/3 - where the 3 was my position in the family.

This was followed by a visit to the village hall to have a gas mask fitted, before it was given to me in the well recognised cardboard box. At school, regular trials took place, to see how quickly we could get our masks on, and be ready when the sirens sounded and the German planes came over!

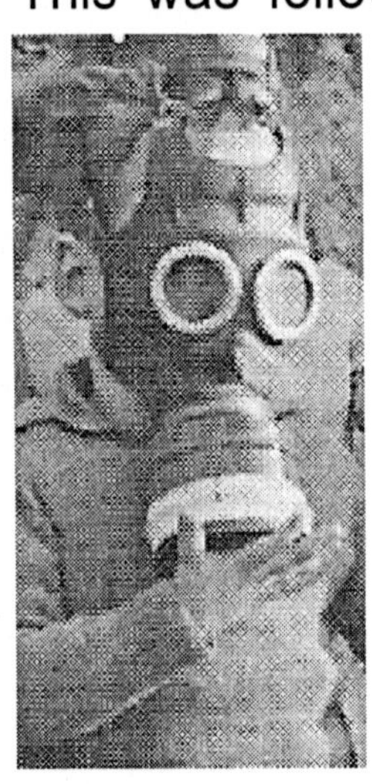

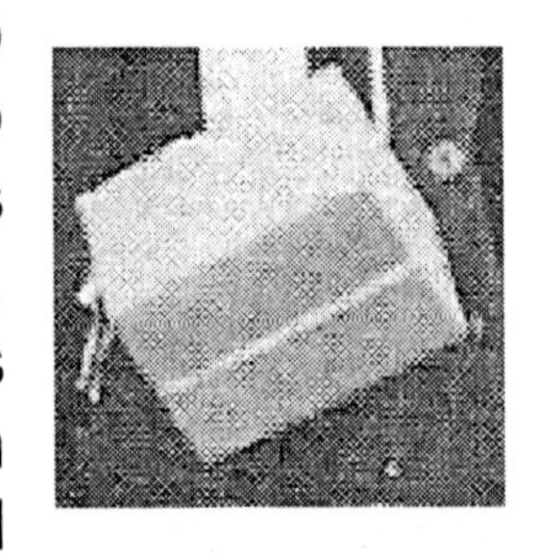

I think that next event in the village, was the forming of the LDV - Local Defence Volunteers. Some of the young men were now being called up into the armed forces, but those left, together with the older men, formed the local group. Their job was to defend the village against the Germans!

We watched this band of "soldiers" drilling at the "Cross Tree" - no guns, no uniforms, only an arm band showing LDV, but there was plenty of enthusiasm, and lots of "mickey" taking by the boy spectators! Dad joined, as he was exempt from "call up", due to his work at Chapple's, where he was transferred from working on cars to maintaining agriculture tractors for the local farms. This work became ever more vital, as the war continued and with the need to produce even more home grown food.

The name changed to the Home Guard and they were issued with uniforms, rifles, bayonets and ammunition. Our house, at times became a mini-arsenal, although the standard issue was five rounds of .303 ammo. / person! Dad was promoted to sergeant, in control of a small section with their dug-out at the corner of the road between our home and the church. There was also a machine-gun post at the top of the field opposite, overlooking the main road. Likewise, there were defence dug-outs circling the village.

All of these H.G. defence points became great places for us to play "soldiers". (I've tried in vain to find out more about the S.W. Home Guard –
No. H52. – However, I could find no records or internet information anywhere.

Government regulations meant that all signposts – mainly finger posts - were removed, so that the enemy would hopefully, have no idea of where they were when they landed! I'm sure that there must have been many friendly troops lost on manoeuvres? Additionally, it was an offence to ring church bells, other than in an emergency. The one occasion came in 1940, when the siren sounded, (It was sited at RAF Odiham) to be followed by a fierce ringing of the local church bells.

The Germans are coming!!! The Germans are coming!!!

Today, I can't think of that time without recalling Dad's Army TV films and Corporal Jones shouting, Don't Panic!! Don't Panic!! - Always a big laugh, but no way did laughing apply back in 1940.
However, I'm sure panic reigned, as Mum and the three of us went to shelter under the stairs and Dad went of to war with his rifle and five rounds of ammunition! - but I never knew!

**S**chooldays during the War

I suppose the biggest change was associated with food. At the Infants School we were able to get a 1/3pint of milk every morning for 1/2d. This was distributed at "milk time", when we were also given a Horlicks tablet - this was followed by play.

That's all I remember until the move to Long Sutton, where we still had milk every day plus school dinners. The meals, which were generally very good, were cooked on site by Mrs Amer from South Warnborough and Mrs Yalden, a local person.

The school had extensive vegetable gardens and a village allotment, so as to be expected the boys became "gardeners". I do believe too much time was spent digging and planting cabbages? - but for us it could be fun - mainly just fooling around! When I became a prefect, I was in charge for a term or two - an absolutely pointless position!

One strange farming technique we watched from the allotment, was ploughing, using steam engines. At each side of the field there was a steam engine, pulling the large plough across the field from one side to the other using thick hawsers. The field had a steep gradient, so I guess it was far too much of an undertaking for tractors of that time! However, worth mentioning as it was the only time I ever saw that form of (roundabout) ploughing! - note the winding drum.

However, by far, the most exciting event happened on another occasion when I was down at the allotments. I can remember every last detail. As usual, our productivity was dismally low, trying to plant rows of Brussels sprout plants between rows of potatoes - how boring?
All of a sudden an aircraft came crashing through the trees, coming to a halt at the lower end of our plot! - Long Sutton, like South Warnborough, was very close to RAF Odiham and therefore we were used to aircraft flying low on landing and take-off, depending on the wind direction - but not this low!!

As keen aircraft spotters, we all knew immediately, it was a Tomahawk, as shown.

Naturally, we were like statues and just stood still with our mouths wide open, wondering what would happen next?

Much to our surprise, the canopy was pushed back and out jumped the pilot, who then came walking casually towards us! He called out - Hi! lads, in an "American" type drawl, - Where is the nearest "call box", I want to get back to camp? Initially, we weren't sure what a call box was! I don't think any of us spoke for a while, but then in unison we pointed up the track to where the village phone box was located!

We found out later that it was a French Canadian squadron who flew the Tomahawks.

It doesn't take much imagination to guess what happened next? Brussels sprout plants forgotten, we rushed down to the plane, and took it in turns to sit in the cockpit and play with the controls - all budding fighter pilots!

Nothing to do with My Story, but a fact which is not very well known, but needs mentioning!

On the old Winchester by-pass there was a bridge called the "Spitfire Bridge". It was very prominent, standing out on a steep incline. On one occasion, a pilot decided he would fly under the bridge - he did, but in doing so, he touched the bridge and lost an outer identification light.

Witnesses said the aircraft was a Spitfire - hence the name stuck!

It was eventually proven that the pilot had been to Eastleigh to pick up his Tomahawk aircraft, which had been undergoing major maintenance. On his way back to Odiham he thought he would have a go!! (Ref. The Canadian Squadron Commander: who wrote at a much later date to the local paper, outlining the true facts and squashing the Spitfire version of the story!)

The name Spitfire, because of its WW2 reputation, is still held in great esteem.

There are many of these fighters still flying, even after sixty years, including several with the Battle of Britain Flight.

Back to My Story - life at school was very similar to most schools - the siren would sound and we would file into one of the two shelters with our gas masks. There was one shelter for the juniors and the other for the seniors. We carried on with some lessons in spite of the semi-darkness - I can't remember the type of lighting, probably a paraffin lamp?

We kept the double doors open for extra light and fresh air, with the headmaster standing outside listening for aircraft.

When they were in the vicinity, there would be a shout, the doors would clang shut and we would wait for the "all clear". We would occasionally see the Gloster Gladiators from RAE Farnborough circling in the distance - as boys we wanted the aircraft to be one type only - you've guessed - Spitfires !

The two shelters were built in the summer of 1940 and that meant we had weeks and weeks at home, OK for fun and games, but unfortunately for me it was in the vulnerable 11+ period with too much time being lost!! – mentioned earlier!

Living in the country, but in the South of England, we were in the midst of military activity. There was continuous army manoeuvres around us, as well as RAF Odiham on one side and the new airfield at Lasham on the other side. As young aircraft enthusiasts we soon learnt to recognise our

own aircraft, both by sight and the sound of the engines. From 1940 onwards this also applied to German aircraft. There were numerous crashes, which as young boys, always attracted our immediate attention - with hindsight, sometimes a very dangerous pursuit with the possibility of live ammunition exploding!!

We just couldn't wait to get into an aircraft that had crash-landed and where it was more serious, we wanted "bits". We soon found it very easy to outwit the guard - just bide our time and in we went - anyway we knew the area and could run faster! - The photo is not of our gang, but typical of what happened!

I remember well the Westland Lysander that crashed in the field next to the Plough Inn, - ammunition all around the aircraft - both live and spent bullet cases - (.303 ammo.). The cases became the ultimate arrow tip, and at their most dangerous when the arrow was used with a catapult!!! By today's rules we would have had scores of ASBO's, dished out by PC Chapman and no doubt, hanging on the bedroom wall!

The Lysanders from Odiham were often used for taking Allied agents to France, as they were an excellent aircraft for landing in, and taking off from the small French fields.

. They were also capable, without landing, of picking-up messages from our agents in France. The briefing and general handling of the agents was carried out at a requisitioned small farm on the far side of Odiham airfield. (I found this out during the 1980's, when I was with a party of Iraqi Air Force Engineering officers on a requested conducted tour of the station.) - During our boyhood it was obviously such a well kept secret and very much a gap in our local knowledge!

Unfortunately, I never heard of any German aircraft crashing in our area. To have reached one it would have meant either, trudging or cycling a long way and we would have done it, had we known!

During 1940/1941 I used to stand in our garden and see the occasional streaking of aircraft across the sky as they were engaged in dogfights. What was really scary, was the large groups of German bombers flying inland - to where I did not know?

One harvest time we found a lot of incendiary bombs, some still live, others spent. It is said, the

Germans did carry out a futile operation to try and catch the harvest fields alight and so destroy the well needed grain? Because of the posters in the village and the lectures at school, we did, on this occasion, report our find to the police.

There were two bomb incidents in the village;
The first was a stick of ten bombs at right angles across the three council houses where I lived. Apparently, there was an army convoy travelling along the road and the lone German bomber dropped its' bombs, missing the troops. However, one bomb hit the house next to ours, knocking off the front corner. Another bomb hit the back of the third house – fortunately, there were no military or civilian casualties.

Dad came to the school soon afterwards to reassure us all that lived in the houses involved, and to explain about the damage to our homes, so that we would not be too shocked when we got home from school.

Of course what did we do immediately after tea? - go searching for shrapnel!

The second was a large unexploded bomb in the field next to, what is called, Ridley's Piece. The whole area was roped off for weeks and weeks as the Sappers dug down to de-commission the bomb! Obviously, nobody went anywhere near the site, in fact it was scary to even venture along Gaston Lane!

Later in the war we heard, and occasionally saw a "Doodle Bug" as it putt- putted over us, on its' way to where?

Another occasion I saw an enemy aircraft, one evening. I was at the back of the house just mooching around, when all of a sudden a Dornier 217 flew over **very, very** low.

Not only did I see the German cross on the fuselage and the swastika on one of the tail fins - a frightening thrill, and to be recounted many times!! - I had an excellent view of two crew members in the cabin. They were looking straight ahead, with no downward glance! If one of them had looked down, I'm sure I would have instinctively shaken my fist! - We always waved or gave a thumbs up to any Allied aircraft in similar circumstances! (Reading was bombed that evening by a lone bomber and I believe it was by the one I had seen earlier!)

My section of the story must seem just a chronicle on aircraft incidents only, but those years were like witnessing a continuous air show?

Lasham airfield also played a big part in our activities. Whereas Odiham was nearly always equipped with various fighter aircraft, including the well known Mustang, Lashams' aircraft included medium bombers such as the Marauders and Mitchells flown by the Dutch and Polish Air Forces. Towards the end of the war these were replaced by the Mosquito and the tank- busting Typhoon.

Our roaming, inevitably, took us through the woods to the Lasham dispersal areas which were not fenced in at all. We dared each other to run up to an aircraft and touch it - what devils we were?

I found out years later that a British married couple, with German connections, living in the Lasham area had been watching aircraft movements for some time and had also been seen on many occasions in these same woods. Apparently they were transmitting this information to Germany from their home. They were eventually arrested and imprisoned as German spies!!!

As the assault on Europe approached, South Warnborough became an area of continuous troop movements. All the boys spent hours with the troops, many of them Canadian. We **lived** well and eventually "the gang" had a full set of equipment from mess tins - vital! -, plus a full set of webbing, gas cape etc. and finally a tin helmet each!

I had a secret hiding place for my "issue" in one of Dad's disused chicken houses. One day we heard that the police were looking for lost equipment!! We hurriedly got rid of ours, where to? - still a "State secret"! But we did keep the mess tins. The rumour was, I believe, started by someone in the village, probably one of our Dads?

The next group to come to the village were the RAF Regiment who camped in the field opposite - what could be better for everybody? All the families in our row of houses benefited from "extra rations" and the boys were adopted by the troops. During this pre D-Day training period we had tremendous fun. We had rides in Canadian Bren gun carriers, a fast light tracked vehicle. "Operated" ack-ack guns, looking for the imaginary enemy plane! and so on! Then D-day came, and I remember the first morning well. As we went off to school, we saw dozens of planes towing gliders, heading for France. Both of our local airfields seemed to be extremely busy that day and for weeks afterwards! Soon the RAF Regiment packed up and they were off to Europe! That Christmas we had a card from one of the men (see below). As you can see, we had nick names - I was called Spud - why? I can't remember, whereas John was called Tich and we do know why! Still, lovely memories!

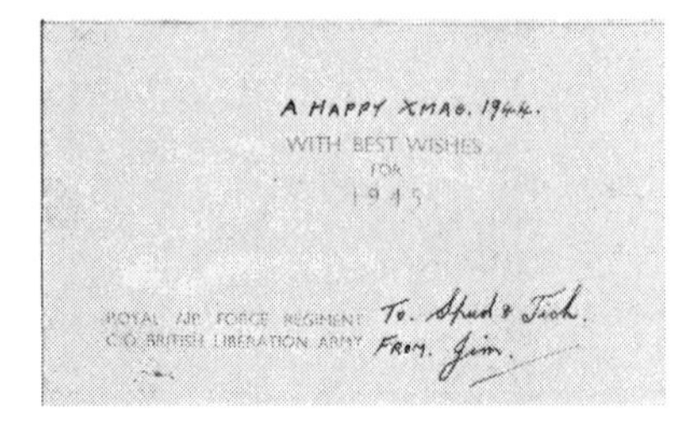


Where Ridley's Piece now exists, the Government erected a batch of buildings for the NFS. The firemen were the pick of the Fire Service and were trained to military standard to support the invasion. Apparently the camp was under strict security prior to D-Day, but due to lack of military enthusiasm the men did not follow the troops over. The Unit was disbanded in late 1944 and the huts used for civilian housing.

The camp at South Warnborough

Herbert Morrison inspects at South Warnborough

We took little interest in the camp as it was non-military!

NOTE: The Ridley Piece council houses were built in1955, the year I completed my 3-year service in the RAF. As a married lad from the village without a house, I was allocated No 16 - which became our second home.
Our "vegetable garden" was immediately above one of the hut concrete foundations with just 3 to 4 ins. of earth cover!

One other notable event was when Italian POW'S were unloaded from an Army lorry every day during the course of one summer. Their job was to help with the harvest on Butler's farm. Their uniform was dark brown with large patches. You can guess the reception they had from the boys, as they marched from the drop-off point at the "cross tree"? - too racist to now put into print! - but we had to let our pent-up feelings be known! The same happened, only worse, when later on, German POW'S, with greyish uniforms, came to the village.

For a young person the feelings associated with war are never eradicated - they stay with you forever. It's very easy to criticise now, but I do know that it is absolutely necessary to live through a war, to fully appreciate these reactions. On the plus side - over the years I've got to know both

Germans and Italians on various lovely holidays and I've made many friends whilst working in both Germany and Italy.

Inevitably, I continued to follow the course of the war in Europe and later in the Far East, listening intently to the radio and reading the newspaper.
Then a came the big day - VE Day - celebrations everywhere!! This was fairly soon followed by the dropping of A-bombs on Japan and immediately - VJ Day - at last the war was over!

I had forgotten to mention the "blackout" and the winter evenings at home leading into the beginning of my teen-age years!
One Government regulation was that a complete black-out of windows was compulsory, with no chinks of light permissible at all. (Dad had also put sticky tape across every pane of glass in all the windows to reduce the affects of blast)
So every Sunday after tea throughout the winter, the thick black-out curtains would be drawn and we would gather round the fire to play games.
Initially, board games such as snakes and ladders, Ludo and draughts were a must. As any of these games progressed, there would inevitably be tears from one of us (even me!) as we were "caught" and it was necessary to start that part of the game again! I know that when we lost we thought they were really horrible games!

Later we graduated to pub games, darts and shove halfpenny. The door in the “front room” became peppered with holes as we missed the dart board and it looked as if it had been attacked by an army of woodworm! Those winter evenings are remembered with great pleasure.

We also played whist, which became one of my favourite games - even today. I eventually went to the whist drive held at the village hall every Wednesday, which was well supported by the villagers.

Saturday nights were not such a pleasure? It was bath night, carried out in a large tin bath (not so bad really), and then it was followed by the compulsory spoonful of “syrup of figs” - I can still taste the horrible stuff!

## **W**ork and Further Study (still war-time)

Then came the time I was to leave school, which was at the end of the term after I reached fourteen years old. I had no idea what I would do? This is where Dad really came to my rescue! At the end of our row of houses was The Never Despair garage, owned by the Richardson family. Dad had occasionally carried out a repair on their car and had got to know Harold Richardson very well!

Consequently, I was given a very junior job at Kelvin Bottomley & Baird in Basingstoke, where he was Production Manager. The factory was a satellite of the main factory and consisted of two storeys of the Eli Lilly Pharmaceutical Co. requisitioned for the expansion of the manufacture of aircraft instruments. In January 1945 it was still busy on war output. The factory was known as Kelvinettes. Somewhere amongst my souvenirs is a certificate thanking me for my contribution to the war effort!

Immediately on starting work, I was given the opportunity to attend the local Education Institute to further my education. I jumped at the chance as I could see myself catching up, on where I had lost out and had been badly let down by Long Sutton School.

The Company gave me time to attend for one day and with two evenings study as well, I was kept very busy with the resulting homework. - Little did I know that this further education would still be going strong when I reached twenty-one and then attending Southampton University - and it also continued throughout my RAF service and when I returned to the Company after the 3-year period!!

Getting to work was a problem as the distance to the factory was about eight miles. The early bus cost about a £1 a week and as my initial wages were about the same, it was necessary for Dad to subsidise me - at least for my canteen lunch! I decided to change the situation by cycling to work, which also gave me more freedom. I did this journey over several years, through periods of terrible weather, including the heavy snowfalls of 1947!

By cycling I was able to cultivate a good wild rabbit "side line". I set wires on my way home and picked up my "catch" in the morning, I did the "necessary" behind the hedge and sold the rabbits when I reached work!

**S**port

I started football by joining the Basingstoke Boys Club who played in the Lads League. In my final

MEMBER of BASINGSTOKE BOYS CLUB
ALSO CUP WINNERS: JOINT TOP GOAL SCORER - 23 GOALS

Basingstoke & District
Lads' Football League
Season 1948-49

THIS IS TO CERTIFY THAT
R. HILLYER.
was a Playing Member
of the BASINGSTOKE BOYS' CLUB. F.C.
Winners of the League Championship

League Chairman

League Hon. Sec.

MAY, 1949

year with them, we won both the league and the cup. In those days I could run very fast and being a natural left footer, I easily got my place in the team as outside left. I scored 23 goals during my final season with them, - never to be repeated!

To play, I had to cycle the 8 miles to Basingstoke and then quite often to a village on the far side, followed by the journey home!

I remember arriving at a match with Tadley (15 miles from home) over ten minutes late, I was called on to the pitch by the Referee and immediately scored! We won the match by one goal!

A photo, medal and certificate from my peak season of playing soccer for over 22years. To keep fit for matches, I also started running or "jogging", which became a natural part of my daily routine, right through to the 2000s and beyond!

## Air Training Corps

During 1945 a local Squadron was formed, with our HQ at RAF Odiham. Although we were officially attached to 1590 Sqdn. at Lord Wandsworth College, Long Sutton, we had no practical connection with them. Our officer was Pilot Officer Jack Southworth, who lived in Greywell. He was a great organiser and arranged for all of our activities to be centred at RAF Station, Odiham.

We started with the inevitable "square bashing" and also covered aspects of navigation, Morse code, Link trainer work (simulated flying) etc. All lectures and training was carried out by RAF personnel.

At the end of each session we high-tailed it to the NAAFI to buy sweets and other items which were very much rationed outside!

One summer we went for a week's camp at RAF Holmsley South, in the New Forest. We lived in typical military bell tents, with four of us in each tent. On the first night there was a violent thunderstorm and our tent leaked so much, that by

morning we were drenched - so much for camping! (albeit we later camped as a family for many years)
However, I did have my first flight - in an Avro York, a 4-engined transport - for freight only! The flight lasted for over 4 hours and as there were no seats we sat on the floor which eventually became an absolute miserable experience!

Brighter times were to come, as RAF Odiham was taken over by the Canadians and several squadrons of Douglas Dakotas moved in (see below). The Dakota had been one of the main transport aircraft operating in all theatres of WW2.

We had flying every Sunday and numerous visits to the PX (NAAFI), - what more could we wish for?
A memorable highlight occurred during one of these flights, when I was invited to sit in the co-pilot's seat and take over the controls! The Dakota was flying over RAE Farnborough and below us was a row of captured German aircraft, including a ME 163 and a ME 262 – both the newer jet aircraft! The pilot said "why don't you take her round again but a bit lower so that you can have a better look!"

Of course, all the time the pilot was leaning over the "trainee"! However, three big cheers for the relaxed attitude of the Canadians, never to be forgotten!

My life in the village continued with study, football and roaming the countryside with my newly acquired Jack Russell terrier, called Nipper. It became superb at catching rabbits in their squats, so we enjoyed the results at home as well as a contribution to my "works business".
In order to get a better social life I ventured into Odiham and joined a Youth Club, where on the first night I met Kate.

In 1952 I enlisted in the RAF on a 3-year engagement and spent the time at RAF St. Athan working on aircraft instruments. I also was able to continue my education at Cardiff University, with maximum support from the RAF.
We got married in 1954 and had our first home in Barry. At the end of my service in 1955, we returned to South Warnborough to move into a new house at No.16 Ridley's Piece,

where we stayed for nearly two years. Here is a photo of Kate looking out of our new home.

We enjoyed nearly sixty years of being together, with many adventures in various parts of the world, the pleasures of bringing up two children and the fun from our four grandchildren.

A painting of South Warnborough in 1929

Two photos, one from the1930's – notice the open school door. The one below was taken in 2007. Many of the cottages are as shown in the 1929 painting.

Below shows a very peaceful winter view of South Warnborough, with the Church as the centrepiece.

I believe this is very much, symbolic of growing up in Our Village, during the period covered by this book.

Ray

# David Oliver

I was born in1933 at New Farm, Froyle Lane, one mile outside the village. My Dad worked on a farm owned by the father of Frank Butler, who had the large farm at the top of Lee's Hill in the village. A Mr. Baggs, was the manager of the farm.

My first memory was being taken to the Manor Park, opposite the council houses along the Alton Road, by my parents. There were a lot of people around and plenty of food spread out on tables. This gathering was to celebrate King George V and Queen Mary's Silver Jubilee and took place in 1935. Later, I had a mug for the Abdication of King Edward V111, followed by one in 1937 for the Coronation of King George V1 and Queen Elizabeth.

A photo of the three mugs, still in tip-top condition!

Growing up on the Farm

From an early age, I spent a lot of time with my Dad around the farm. It was always full of fun and adventure. One of my earliest photos is with his horse, which was a real “gentle giant”.

The next photo shows all the crew just after another corn rick had been built, with little me, in front of my Dad. The other boys would have been either stooking the sheaves of corn or leading a horse with a loaded wagon from the field to the rick, The wage for the boys was 1d or 2d an hour.

As you can see, that as I get older, I'm allowed to sit astride my Dad's horse. Sometimes he would stop at our house to let me ride on the cart and I would feel so proud sitting on the cart and being pulled along by this heavy horse.

Our Neighbours

As I grew older, I got to know the Charlton family next door. There was Barbara who was my age and Jo, two years older. Three others were much older still! The Shirley family, who lived further down the road towards the village, was also a large family – some older and others younger. So I did have plenty of playmates to grow up with, plus a baby sister, Joy who had just arrived!

School

I started attending the village school in 1938, Mrs. Bowie was the only teacher.

My mother used to take me to school on the back of her bicycle with my baby sister Joy strapped in a wicker basket fitted to the cycle handlebars. This lady's cycle was so easy to ride, it had large wheels and was low geared – this type of bike was called "a sit up and beg bike". The road to school had a large dip in it and going down the slope, Mum would pedal quite fast. I would shout – faster Mum, faster, in an effort to try and reach the top of the hill the other side, if not, off we got and walked.

When I became older I walked to school with the Charlton and Shirley families. We often got very wet on this long journey to school and we were

very fortunate that the school had a large cast iron stove with a wire guard around it for protection.
I am in the front row of our school photo, second from the right, in this photo taken in 1939. The white house in the background is still there today.

I was six years old when the war started and I can remember seeing one dogfight high in the sky, but I can't tell you the result as both aircraft disappeared from sight. Our fighter planes would use Froyal Lane, from the village to the "Bumpers" for low flying practice. This lane was two or three miles long, with shrubs and young trees forming a wide hedgerow on either side of the road. Our house was about the centre point of the hedgerow stretch and at first we would hear the aircraft engine as the aircraft hopped up and down. We covered our ears to deaden the noise as it roared overhead and when it had passed over we would look to see if any chimney pots were missing! We called this hedge hopping!
Twice, when walking home from school we found a plane had crashed, or belly flopped in the hedge row and a policeman stood guard by the plane.

## Life around our Home and the Farm

On Sunday mornings I would attend Sunday school in the village hall. When it was a nice summer evening the whole family, sometimes with relatives, would walk to the Bumpers (pub) for a drink. The young ones would have a glass of lemonade and a packet of Smiths Crisps – we thought this was great fun!

I can remember that once, with my sister Joy, we went in the milk cart with our Dad to deliver two milk churns to the Bumpers. We loved the horse and cart rides and as the horse was ex-army, it was obedient and so we were able to trot along the road with ease. Other enjoyable rides were when we went to Alton Brewery to collect waste grain to feed the animals on the farm.

Tuesday was always special in Alton as it was "cattle market day". Occasionally, we would take some of my young tame rabbits to sell, or buy day old chicks to rear. These would eventually supply us with eggs to eat and to make cakes. Any chicks that grew into cock birds would be fattened for the

table.

One Saturday morning, I went off to see my Dad, who was ploughing a field with his team of three horses pulling a two-furrowed plough. This was a very arduous job, both for the ploughman and the horses, with very little rest during a day's work!

Nearby, where we were ploughing, the huntsmen and hounds were chasing a fox. Dad's normal procedure on finishing work (12.00 on Saturdays) was to unhitch the horses and then let them stroll back to the water trough on their own. On every other occasion this has worked so naturally, but as they started off today, so the huntsman blew his horn – as you probably guessed the **ex-military horse** was away, **charging** after the hounds and really enjoying itself! Luckily a huntsman caught the horse and returned it to us.

I'm a little older in this photo of me with my Grandad Oliver. He lived with us and was liked by all the children on the farm. We would go with him for long walks, which we called our "nature walks".

One day he took us to a large field where two traction engines were ploughing. This is what we saw – one engine either side of the field facing sideways to each other and both attached to an 8-furrow reversible plough via a steel wire rope. A man sat on the plough seat and his job was to set the depth of the plough and to steer it from one side of the field to the other when pulled by each engine in turn. The cable wound round a drum under the engine. The engine drivers used a system of whistle toots to indicate when it was time to move further up the field.

I remember Grandad making a telephone out of two treacle tins. He punched a hole in the bottom of each tin using a nail and then they were linked with a piece of string and a knot tied in each end. One of us would put a tin to our ear to listen and the other would talk loud into the other. We swopped from ear to mouth as we held a conversation!

Another simple toy was made with a cotton reel, one elastic band and two used matchsticks. First Grandad would cut "V" shapes around the outside rims of the cotton reels, break one of the matchsticks in about half and then affix it to one end of the elastic band, before feeding the band through the centre of the reel. Wind up the band with the longest stick, place the reel on the ground and it will move along dragging the longer stick –

using your imagination a lot of fun can be had with such a fantastic machine!

We used old bicycle tyres as hoops and would run along beside a tyre to see how long we could keep it rolling before it hit the bank or went into a ditch.

Always, we had to make our own fun, using any scrap materials we could find, but we were never bored or without friends to enjoy any of the games.

## Long Sutton School

When I reached eight years old it was time to change schools. Every day, regardless of the weather, I walked the mile to the village with the Charlton and Shirley families. We met the other children at the "cross tree", to be taken to Long Sutton School by Guy Freeman in his Ford V8 shooting break. It was fitted out with bench seats and sometimes had to make three journeys, depending on the number of children. This was our school transport throughout the war years!

Miss Hoyes was my teacher and I liked her teaching.

I remember one day when I, as the soldier and Barbara Charlton as the pretty maiden had to stand up in front of the class and act the play –

Soldier, soldier, will you marry me
in all your fine clothes?

I cannot marry you today my
pretty maiden, as I have not
got my musket with me!
(repeated, adding fife, then drum)

My final line was,
I cannot marry you today my pretty
maiden with my musket, fife and drum
My Wife Won't Let Me

1942 brought about many changes in our farming community. First, our Grandad passed away, a sad loss to us all. Then, because the war needed more and more men and women, it affected most families. Both Jack Shirley and George Charlton were called up into the Army and Hazel Charlton joined the Auxiliary Territorial Service.

Mother took in a **conscientious objector** lodger to work in the dairy, but he didn't stay long. The next objector was different and stayed for some time, carrying out different tasks on the farm.

Dad joined the Civil Defence and Mother joined the Woman's Institute at the village hall. She also joined the Mother's Union.

All the children helped the war effort by collecting rose hips from the hedgerows, which were sent off to make syrup. We would gather acorns and sell them to the farmers for their pigs. I helped pick gooseberries and black currants from our garden, so that Mother could make jam. One day we went hunting for wild strawberries – a very small, but with an extremely sweet taste. I had spent a long time picking a lovely bowl full, when I tripped and the fruit went flying! With tears in my eyes, I was made to search amongst the grass and leaves to pick up as many as possible!

Another time, when I was playing outside our gate, I picked and ate some other brightly coloured fruit. Little did I know they were poisonous (lords and ladies). Mother noticed my red lips and when I told her what I had been eating, I was immediately given a half bottle of "syrup of figs" to try and get the poison from my system. I was unwell for some time, but I do believe that her prompt action saved my life!

It was now time for me to join Mr. Wilmot's class and I was not looking forward to it at all – was it because I was a slow learner or because of his reputation? He walked between the desks with his swishy cane ready to strike any pupil not doing their work properly – no one escaped! However this discipline made you concentrate on every lesson.

The vegetables grown in the school gardens were prepared and cooked by the "dinner ladies". It was the older boys who looked after the gardens, as part of their gardening lesson. All the gardening tools were kept in one of the air raid shelters and had to be thoroughly cleaned after use – a nasty job! I do not remember going into a shelter during an air raid.

Later as the war advanced and food became scarcer, the Government introduced **Dig for Victory.** The school was given another large garden so now all the boys had to help to grow food. Some of the surplus vegetables were stored for the winter and the fruit was put into large screw top jars, a process called "bottling". I remember peeling and slicing apples into rings, threading a piece of string through the rings and hanging them in front of the window to dry. Another subject I enjoyed very much was woodwork.

Just outside of the playground was a clump of very tall elm trees. Jimmy James and me would climb to the top and play at Tarzan, swinging through the branches. One day Jimmy fell, but fortunately no bones broken, just badly bruised! Because I enjoyed climbing trees, I continued, until one day my Dad thought that the large swelling on my neck was due to all the climbing?

Off to Reading Hospital to have a large gland removed, then after a week I was sent to Battle Hospital for three weeks convalescence. There I was taught how to play draughts and also spent a lot of time doing puzzles. I did come home with something that was to cause me some more pain! – **nits** - a head full of them. Mother washed my hair in liquid paraffin to kill the nits, then cut my hair very short and using a fine tooth comb, dipped in boiling water, soon got rid of them – what a relief!

My memories of D-Day

I only have two memories of D-Day as we travelled along the Long Sutton road to school. We could see part of Odiham airfield, which seemed to be covered with aircraft. The airfield was never hit by German bombs, which does seem very surprising.

After school, when I walked along to the village shop, by chance, I met John Hillyer. He took me along to the Manor park, opposite his house, to see the Royal Canadian Air Force. I only remember walking between the tents for a while, then, I wandered back to the village shop to collect three of their own baked loaves. Sometimes after school, when we were hungry, we would buy four buns at 1/4d each (total 1d), to eat on the way home. I also collected our milk which had been left at the Woodrow's house – at the bottom of Froyle Lane.

Mr. Woodrow was the gamekeeper on the farm where we lived. When he held a pheasant shoot, the boys could get a job as beaters - and be paid!

SWH 19 THE VILLAGE, SOUTH WARNBOROUGH.

During the winter months my Mother and Mrs. Charlton took me to the weekly whist drive at the village hall. I remember long before D-Day, when we were on our way home we would see the long beams of the searchlights looking for German bombers and the anti-aircraft shells exploding. Twice we saw the red glow in the sky coming from large fires – probably in London.

Now that I was older I spent more time with my Dad on the farm. I would take his tea (and mine) to wherever he was working, sit round with the men and enjoy our tea – it was like having a picnic!

The old horse was now used for driving the elevator. It was connected to a long wooden pole and by going round and round it turned the gears on the elevator that took the hay from the ground to the man on the rick. My job was to keep the horse going round and round.

The schools were given an extra two weeks holiday to help gather in the harvest. I would help in the harvest field by putting sheaves of corn into stooks, where it stood to dry out before being collected and built into ricks. The farm's Land Army girl was Mave Smith from the village.

Italian prisoners of war came to work on the farm. They were always busy making things, such as baskets from willows, which they sold to the ladies. They made rings from silver 3d and 6d coins. My mother had a ring made with her initials etched on the outside. It is one of my sister Joy's most treasured keepsakes.

………. even more Work and Play

That year's summer holiday was my best, as I was able to lead the horses with loaded wagons. One day, completely unaware, I stopped the Shire horse and his front hoof was covering a hole in the ground – it was a wasp's nest! The horse kept stamping its foot and I was told to move away from the nest. The wasps had been stinging the soft part of the horse's hoof (the frog). Another day I had just brought in a wagon loaded with sheaves and was positioning it by the rick when Dad shouted – German bombers! – and as they came flying low over the fields, we all got ready to run for cover!. Luckily they were on their way home after a bombing raid. I heard later, that bombs had been dropped near Odiham and Lasham airfields and one in the village!

Autumn half term was potato picking time and most children took part. The system was to be spaced out between markers, with a bucket and when full, put the potatoes into hessian sacks. Of course, the most natural boy-type action was to try and shorten your own working length as you periodically moved the marker! I was next to Joe Charlton and his length became shorter at my expense – he was several years older than me, so Mother had to sort him out! - so no further problems.

As we were neighbours, I played with Joe a lot and got involved in making all sorts of things, including using hacksaw files and a red hot poker to make rings from Perspex – taken from crashed aircraft canopies. We made a go-cart from old pram wheels, a piece of wood to sit on and a length of string for steering. We had great fun playing with our new machine!

The most dangerous "fun" was when we found two live rounds of ammunition. We found a post with a hole the right size to take the round. Using a nail and hammer we struck the end until there was a bang and the bullet went whizzing across the field! On one of my visits to the village, to collect the milk, I met Tommy Goodchild and a few more boys. Opposite the Woodrow's house there was a garden with some apple trees and we decided to do some scrumping. Squeezing through the hedge I put my hand on a partly broken bottle – oops! – a large cut appeared on my wrist. Tom took me to his house and his Mum bandaged it to stop the bleeding. I needed five stitches and I was told a sinew was slightly cut. Luckily it healed successfully and I then vowed no more scrumping.

## Changes to Our Family

We now had an increase in our family with the birth of my sister Iris. Also, we took in our three cousins from Southampton, whose house had been badly bombed. Their father was in the Services and their mother felt they would be safer with us. They stayed with us for three/four months and whilst they were here they attended Long Sutton School.

### **N**ew Excitements

This started when my Dad bought a second hand bicycle from the Hillyers in the village. I remember my Dad running along side of me and holding the back of the saddle so that I wouldn't fall off. As I began to go faster my Dad had let go and when I realised this, I wobbled and ended up in a bed of stinging nettles. From then on I taught myself to ride – of course, I now wanted to ride into the village to join the Air Training Cadets run by Ray Amer. The meetings were normally held in the Manor stables, but on nice evenings we had activities in the park at the back of the Manor, next to Froyle Lane. Ray took us on a weekend camp to a field along Ford Lane. We pitched our tents up a slope away from the sheep dip and underground springs. All the cooking was done on the camp fire and we had a really good time. You can imagine that by the time we arrived home we were very, very dirty, but happy!

..... back to Farming

It was now time to carry out the threshing of the corn. It was quite a sight to see the traction engine trundling through the lanes, pulling the thrashing tackle and puffing out dirty black smoke under its heavy load. When the machinery was set up one of the men would put up the compulsory wire netting around the site to stop the rats and mice from escaping. As the rick became lower, the vermin would leave and that is when the boys would be waiting with their sticks. It was essential to tie a piece of string around the bottom of your trousers, to stop them climbing up the inside of your trouser leg! It was good fun, as not many got away and we were doing our bit for the war effort!

Some winter moonlit nights, Dad and I would go off to saw up fallen trees or branches for firewood. We used a cross-cut, where Dad was on the main handle and I was pulling the small handle. It was hard work sawing, backwards and forwards through the wood, and I always "**slept like a log**" after an evenings work.

Dad collected the wood next day using his young Shire horse and cart, and the wood would become part of our winter fuel.

Now I had a brother Roy and the war had come to an end. The Christmas following was the first one I can remember. We hung some of mother's stockings next to the fireplace and when we awoke in the morning, all four of us found a full stocking at the foot of our bed. Each one contained fruit, a reading book, drawing and crayoning books etc. and of course sweets, which were rationed. It was still hard times and we had to be very careful.

**S**adly, in 1946, our Dad died and from then on our lives changed dramatically. I was the eldest and, mother now shared her decisions with me. Her brother from Southampton was a great help to us. As we lived in a tied house we knew we would soon have to vacate our home. Mr. Baggs, the farm manager, decided we could swap houses with the Shirley family as a temporary measure, until we could arrange other accommodation. Mother told me she would do everything possible to keep her four children with her.

She wrote a few pleading letters. One response was to live at the Manor stables. The Parish Council had at that time, decided to convert the NFS huts into family homes and we were allocated one. This is how we came to live in the village at, what is known, as Ridley's Piece. I was now thirteen years old and trying to cope with our loss, but it was nice to see Mother happy again. She rallied the four of us to overcome the past and to look to the future.

We set to and created our own veggie patch. At school, Mr. Wilmot the headmaster, was very sympathetic towards me and had given me space to settle down. However, he now hoped I would now start to concentrate on my lessons, which I did. I was beginning to like school, with more gardening and woodwork lessons. I was also in the school cricket team and although we had to play football, I did not like the game.

Mr. Wilmot left the school and a lady teacher took over. Then at 14 years old, I was, with some other boys, transferred to Odiham Boys School. Our transport was by the Nancy Bus Service.

## Life in the village

Roley White lived two huts from us and he and I became great friends. One of our hobbies was birds egg collecting and sometimes we would hide and study a birds behaviour. The skylark was the most fascinating to watch, for after a rain shower had past over and the sun appeared, it would rise high in the sky singing merrily.

Often Roley would take me to see his grandparents at Tunworth. It was good fun walking through the woods with his Grandad, who was a gamekeeper. One evening, he took us to find a nightjars nest and after waiting to hear the sound of the nightjar, we found its nest on the ground – another egg for our collection. On the way home we heard a vixen fox calling to her mate, which, for the first time, I found very scary!

Len Digweed became a frequent visitor to our place, although I knew him at New Farm, where his wife had died. Mother married him

Len became a very supportive step-father to all four of us.

We would play cricket wherever there was a grassy space. I would play for the village when they were short, but Roley, who was a better cricketer than me, was picked more often. I would then do the scoring. The team played in the Manor Park, next to Alton Road.

One of our evening enjoyments was to listen to Dick Barton, Special Agent on the radio. Each episode was for fifteen minutes and broadcast Monday to Friday.

Six new Council Houses were built in Froyle Lane and No. 6 became ours. Here is a lovely and treasured photo of the four of us in the garden.

Joy, David, Roy and Iris.

Roley,s family moved in next door at No.5. We both joined the Church choir with John Hillyer and attended morning and evening services.

Mr. Oldfield, the Rector paid us 1d for each attendance.

A Youth Club was held in the village hall where all sorts of indoor games were played. When Captain Roskill became our youth leader, he organised a weekend for George Spreadborough, John Hillyer and myself at a disused Naval base in Havant. We joined other groups to discuss how to run a youth club successfully. From the meeting, activities such as table tennis, boxing and dance lessons were introduced. We even held dances. The Club went on for a few years.

At fifteen years I left school and my first job was working on Captain Roskill's smallholding at Blounce Farm. I first worked on the horticulture side, where a lot of the produce grown was sold to the public. This is where I learnt to drive a tractor. A dairy herd of Jersey cows was slowly built up and I then started to deliver milk to the village and to Powntley Copse. I used a 500cc BSA motorcycle outfit, purchased from the Green Garage. It had a large box fitted to the side-car, for carrying the milk. Owen Tyler took me for driving lessons on his 600cc Panther. The next photo is taken from our garden and shows the back view of the Green Garage. This is followed by one of Owen Tyler standing in the doorway of his garage. Peter Cripps, one of the two mechanics is shown standing behind the other, Les Williams is on a Triumph motorcycle.

INSURANCE

Here is a photo of Owen taking part in a rally on his Scott motorcycle.

John Hillyer was the first of us to get a motorcycle and with Roley on his pillion, they would pull me on my push bike into Alton for the cinema. On our bicycles, a gang of us cycled to Frensham Pond for a swim. During our return journey we got caught in a terrific thunderstorm and without anywhere to shelter, we cycled bare-chested into Alton. We bought some refreshment at the shop where Sheila Cameron worked and dried out before we left for home.

It was now time for me to do my National Service. Here I am with my step brother John.

After I left the Army, I became interested in

motorcycling and started with a BSA 250cc. I later graduated to a Triumph 500cc, both coming from The Green Garage. The garage was extremely popular with the village lads as well as the surrounding area. Motorcycling gave us so much pleasure and freedom in those early years.

This concludes my memories from events of living in the village of South Warnborough for 26 years.

**Roy Oliver**

However, I will include some of my brother Roy's adventures, which I still remember well as he loved to copy the older boys. One trick we did was to swing a pail of water in a complete circle over our heads without spilling a drop. Roy tried it with a pail of milk (possibly egged on by us) and hesitated when the pail was above his head with the inevitable result! So as expected he was in real trouble from mother.

Another mishap was when Roy tried walking on the village pond railings. He got half way round, slipped and ended up with one leg either side the railing! He was in such pain with tears running down his face that he rushed home. Mother took a quick look and applied a towel soaked in cold water to ease the pain. No more stunts for Roy!

Later Roy, Alan Hide and Kenny Breadmore, formed a skiffle group. Kenny on guitar, Alan had a wooden washboard where the ribbed face of the board was rubbed with a spoon to give a musical sound. Roy provided base, which consisted of a wooden tea chest to act as the sound box, with a broom handle protruding and a piece of wire tightly strung between the handle and the tea chest. During the period skiffle was popular the group, together with many others, did enter a competition in Reading.

Roy, who was quite tall, played for the village football team. His success as their goalkeeper enabled him to play for the club over many years.

# Amy "Sue" Shirley

I was born on 5$^{th}$ March 1929, at Tile Barn Cottages, between South Warnborough and Upton Grey. My parents, Elisabeth (nee Charmin) and Jesse Shirley had 11 children, of whom I was the 6$^{th}$.

My brothers and sisters were, in order:
Richard, born 1921 and died 1930
Thomas (known as Harry), born 1922 and died 1972
Ellen (known as Peg), born 1924 and died 1986
Jack, born 1925 and died 1995
Bob, born 1927
Amy (known as Sue), born 1929
May, born 1931
Margaret, born 1935
Arthur, born 1936 and died 1958
Rose, born 1939
Peter, born 1942

I was christened Amy in South Warnborough Church, but my Granny (Jesse's mother) refused to call me Amy and said she would always call me Susie.

My father, Jesse Shirley, worked as a carter, for Mr Tuck of Tile Barn Farm. Understandably, my mother Elisabeth remained at home to care for their large family.

In October 1930, when I was just over 18 months old, our family moved to No 3 New Farm Cottages, South Warnborough, a two-up, two-down cottage with very basic amenities. Water had to be drawn from an outside tap, baths were taken in a tin bath in front of the open fire (which had two bars above it from which to hang pots) in the kitchen, cooking took place on a coal-fired range which had to be 'blacked' each morning, and the children all shared two double beds in one of the upstairs rooms, boys in one bed and girls in the other. My parents slept in the other room. Washing was boiled in a copper close to the fireplace, and the flat iron was stood to heat on a small shelf at the front of the range.

Life was hard, but family life was busy and well-ordered. The girls helped in the house with the cleaning, and the boys helped their father in the garden. I remember a wonderfully stocked vegetable patch with red and green gooseberries, red, white and black currants, rhubarb, lettuces, radishes and spring onions. No doubt there were rows of potatoes and cabbages too. No modern fertilizers then – the wood ash from the fire was combined with the contents of the privy and placed weekly in the bottom of a trench in the vegetable garden. The garden contained apple trees too; a Bramley, a Codling and an eating apple. My father used to gather the fruit with great care and place them in a tea chest interleaved with newspaper, and then closed up with a lid. This was opened on Christmas Day, when all the children could look forward to a nice fresh apple.

Our neighbours in No 4 New Farm Cottages were Reg and Louie Oliver. Reg and my dad worked together as carters for Mr Baggs of New Farm. In 1947, when I was just 18, I remember poor Reg suffering from cancer and, in a fit of depression, committed suicide. He was missing for several days, and the police searched everywhere including the well at the bottom of the garden, but eventually it was found that he had heaved away the stone slabs from the septic tank and drowned. I remember Mrs Oliver (who was later to marry our other neighbour Mr Digweed who lived at No 1) then raising her family (of two boys and two girls) on her own, bicycling miles to take in washing to earn a few shillings, and bravely carrying on. I always admired her courage and we remained lifelong friends until Mrs. Digweed's death in 2005, aged 97.

One of my earliest memories was being taught, to knit, aged 4, by my mother, using the wooden skewers saved from the Sunday joint, and string.

With my sisters, we would make dishcloths for use at home. My mother always made us one cooked meal a day and we never went hungry, and we walked everywhere. Toys and games were only given at Christmas and these would be shared. Otherwise we invented our own games and played endlessly outside in the garden or in the road.

At the age of 5, I started at South Warnborough village school, where there was one classroom, and one teacher for 20 children. On one side of the classroom was a long bench and tables for the smallest children, and on the other were tiny desks and chairs. Lessons, from 9am until 4pm, were reading, writing and arithmetic and were all taught by Mrs Bowie. She always treated the children as though they were her own, and consequently she was much loved. She also held handwork classes and I remember knitting a red jumper, having to stop at 4pm to go home, starting it up again the next day, but knitting in the wrong direction, unfortunately leaving a hole. Kindly, Mrs Bowie unpicked all the stitches and put it right.

Other children who were there at the same time as me were: Roy Adlam, Jean and Ray Amer, Evelyn Benfield, Derek and Rosemary Blake, Freda and Audrey Bristow, Doris and Gordon Digweed, Ray Hillyer, Peggy and Daphne Knight,

Frances and Winnie Lay, Ron and Reg Silver and their cousin Joyce Silver, and Rose Spreadborough (Jimmy's sister). We were never cold as the classroom was heated with two combustion stoves, one at the front of the room and the other at the back. At break-times we were given the regulation ⅓ pint of milk and we took our own sandwiches for lunch, with Mrs Bowie providing us with blue enamel plates with a dark blue border, and blue mugs for cocoa. Washing up was done by Mrs Bowie, with the older children wiping and the little ones putting away. There was perfect, happy order, but a big change was to come when we left at 8 years old to go to Long Sutton School.

In September 1937, I moved to Long Sutton School, built in 1929 by Lord Wandsworth College. I joined Class 1, the infants, where our teacher was Mrs Fry. I remember being taught raffia and basket work, and scripture, along with reading, writing and arithmetic. One day a week, all the children did gardening, with the boys digging and the girls planting. My next teacher was Miss Russ who taught needlework, and I remember learning fine pulled threadwork to make borders around handkerchiefs. It took hours! The head teacher was Mr Wilmott, who taught in the 'top room', and he was very strict. If pupils misbehaved, they would be "beaten", and the parents would be told.

In many homes, the father would probably "beat" them again once they got home. Consequently, we learned very quickly to behave!

Between the ages of 8 and 9, I attended Sunday school at St Andrew's, getting 2$^{nd}$ prize of a hymn and prayer book in 1938 for good attendance.

Once a year, there was an outing for mothers and children to Bognor. We went in a charabanc. I particularly remember wearing a red gingham dress, and being given 3d. vouchers which we could spend on the swing boats, or buy candy floss or peanuts.

When I was 9 years old, I would go with my two brothers, Bob and Jack, to Odiham to do the Saturday shopping, taking the 7.30am Ruby Queen bus for 1d. fare. We called on Mr Rushton at Radio House with accumulators to be re-charged, Mr Carter the butcher in the Bury, and Mr Hands for shoe repair materials for our father who mended all our shoes at home. There were regular instalments to be paid in to the haberdashery shop towards future needs, and finally the general shopping at the International Stores. Then we had to **walk** back and be home by 12 noon! Noticing the regular trio trudging wearily back each Saturday morning, a kindly Mrs McCann, who lived halfway between Odiham and South Warnborough, took pity on us and gave us lemonade. Seeing that we were worried and might get into trouble, she promised us "I won't say anything if you don't say anything"!

During the holidays, we were not allowed into the village, nor to play in the fields. However, we could **work** in the fields for 1d. per hour, either stacking corn sheaves into stooks, turning hay or, if one of us was lucky, leading the horse, which helped to operate the elevator carrying corn sheaves up to the corn rick.

I was also trusted to take out teas to the farmer Mr Baggs and his friend, and for this Mr Baggs would buy me a pair of John White shoes and two pairs of stockings which would last me through the winter. And because I was so thin, his very jolly wife used to give me a pint glass of milk and a cake or bun.

Aged 11½, I clearly recall sitting in the classroom of Long Sutton School on the afternoon of Friday, 18th October, 1940. It was 3.30pm, and suddenly the roar of German bombers was heard fast approaching from the south.

"Everybody, under your desks!" ordered her schoolmistress Miss Russ, and so everyone obediently dived for cover. The bombers roared overhead, heading for the Aerodrome (now RAF Odiham) with their deadly load, but they overshot it, and instead dropped 4 bombs all along Odiham high street, demolishing houses and shops, and killing several people.

At 12 years old, I joined a group of about 8 Girl Guides, with two friends Gladys and Hazel Charlton. The group was run by Mrs Pilkington at South Warnborough Manor. As well as all the usual things learned with the Guides, I remember happy times spent making camp fires in the copses off Gaston Lane, cooking sausages and baked beans. Those copses have now gone, Nash Meadows and Ridleys Piece having taken their place.

After leaving school, I left my home in South Warnborough to go into "service" with a family in Upton Grey village.

This photo is of me when I was sixteen.

Later I volunteered to join the ATS for a two year period and did my training at Guildford, which lasted two months. I was then sent to Gresford near Wrexham and later to Larkhill, where I was attached to the Royal Artillery. The badge "Ubique", meaning "everywhere", is pinned to my tunic.

I thoroughly enjoyed my time in the service and made so many friends. One of them lives near Preston and I still keep in touch with her. I would have stayed in the ATS, having changing its name to the WRACS, but unfortunately my mother became seriously ill and I had to leave the service to look after her.

# Don Silver

My parents were Son and Ettie Silver and I had two sisters. The older one was Joy and the younger one Jean, who was my twin. We were all born at No. 3 Alton Road.

Life in South Warnborough from 1930 was quite basic, but family life for children was very happy.
I went to the infant school in the village from 1935 to 1940. Our head teacher was Miss Bowie who lived two doors from us in Alton Road. The school had outside toilets and a large cast iron stove to heat the whole room.

When we reached the age of ten we transferred to the junior/senior school at Long Sutton, where we stayed until the leaving age of fourteen.
Our head master was Mr. Wilmot and the other two members of staff were Miss Russ and Miss Hoyes, who played the piano. We had school dinners which we all enjoyed and were cooked by Mrs. Amer.
We were taken to school by Mr. Freeman's shooting brake, which held about ten children. He also owned the village shop.
Every day after lessons were finished, Roy Adlam and I would collect Mr. Wilmot's motor cycle from the garage and with one of us riding and the other

pushing it, we took it and put it on its stand outside the school gate. It was then ready for him to ride home to Fleet.
We spent a lot of our time during our senior years in the school garden growing vegetables to help the war effort. This considerably cut down the time we could spend on academic subjects! We had swimming lessons in the Vicarage pool. Revd. Forbes was in charge of the pupils and he helped those with swimming difficulties by holding them above the water with a noose on a long pole.

One day, I think it was in 1942, we were in the school playing field, when we saw something fall from a Lysander aircraft. It looked like a large piece of metal and turned out to be a door from the aircraft – fortunately it did not fall near anyone. The RAF collected it later in the day.
During 1940, a German bomber, possibly being chased by an RAF fighter, released a stick of ten bombs, of which one hit and badly damaged No.4 Alton Road taking out the front wall of the house. The damage was so extensive that the stairs and the bed could be seen from the road. Luckily, there were no casualties and the occupants moved into No. 3. The remainder of the bombs fell into the fields at the front and back of our houses.
There were many bombs dropped in the area at different times, some setting the corn fields alight.

Many people helped put these fires out. During 1944 Street Farm House was taken over by the RCAF and we had many happy times playing baseball in the field next to the house.

One of our activities during springtime was to pick wild flowers in the lanes and sell them to passers-by. I also spent many hours with my uncle Percy (Feller) Silver who lived at No.4, next door. He was my father's younger brother and had two sons, Reg and Ron.

We spent many hours catching rabbits and he had an arrangement with Frank Butler at Dogmersfield Park to control the rabbit population eating the crops grown for food. I would cycle with

him to the Park to help him and in the autumn also picked up potatoes left over from the harvesting. He would hang the rabbits over the handlebars of his bicycle and they would be sold to the local butcher for sale in his shop to the general public.
My uncle had lost his left hand in a shooting accident and so was unable to join the army during the war.
We would cycle together in all weathers to nearby villages, to "partner" whist drives. I would shuffle and deal the cards for him as he was unable to take his turn. He played by balancing his cards on his injured forearm.
On one occasion, we queued all night outside the Oval cricket ground in London, to watch England play Australia. This remains a highlight of my early life.

I was very much a lone child, with my sisters being company for each other. When I was ten or eleven I spent many hours climbing the lime trees in the avenue at South Warnborough trying to catch jackdaws so that I could teach them (unsuccessfully) to talk. On one occasion on climbing a tree at dusk and looking into a nest, I was confronted by three pairs of eyes looking at me. I nearly fell out of the tree in fright at this ghastly sight. The eyes belonged to three baby barn owls waiting for their mother to bring them supper. I came down the tree a lot quicker than when I had climbed up!

My father was in the army during the war and this photo was taken so that he always had a picture of me with him.

My uncle would catch the rabbits by putting ferrets into the burrows to flush them out. The ferrets were kept in cages at the bottom of the garden and were fed on bread and milk. My cousin and I would walk to Long Sutton to see smallholder Chico Yalden, who would give us bread for the ferrets. We would always ask for a currant loaf "for the dog" and scoff it on the way home – so Dash the dog went without!

We all sang in the choir at SW church. I can remember coming out of choir practice and throwing snowballs at the church clock. Winters were much colder in those days, with a lot more snow and windows would frost over at night.

I played football for Long Sutton and the following photo shows me with my cousin Reg, already for a game. We played in the field behind the school.

In the years that followed, cricket became my main sport and for one period, five members of the Silver family played in the team.

In 1944 I left school and went to work in the NAFFI stores at RAF Odiham. It was heavy work as all stores came in bulk and had to be unloaded by hand, including sides of bacon. However, I did get to taste peanut butter for the first time. One of the large drums was damaged and I was able to sample the contents! The RCAF was very well fed and even had their own ice cream parlour, which unfortunately, was out of bounds to civilians.

One day we were in the church when the noise of aircraft was so loud that we went outside to see what was happening? There were formations of

aircraft towing gliders that seemed to change direction as they reached the church. I think they were taking part in the Arnhem raid.
I spent a lot of time at Lasham airfield, which is still open today, mainly for gliding. I would cycle up there and stay all day watching aircraft movements, including loading bombs on to planes. There were Typhoons, Mosquitoes and a Dutch squadron of B-25's attached to the RAF. This was all in preparation for D-Day.

In 1946 I joined the ATC and after my training enjoyed several flights, which included trips in Airspeed Oxford, Dakota and Dominie aircraft. I was very interested in aircraft recognition and scored 98% when I did my National Service in the RAF, from 1948-1950.

see certificate >

ROYAL AIR FORCE.

**Efficiency Certificate**

*This Certificate is given in recognition of the exceptional high average obtained in*

Aircraft Recognition Ex. A.T.C.

*during Recruit Training at No. 4 Recruit Training Centre, R.A.F. Station Wilmslow.*

Percentage Obtained 98%

A.C. II Silver.

*Flight Entry Date* 16th September, 1948.

*Flight Pass Out Date* 10th November, 1948.

*Group Captain.*

*Officer Commanding R.A.F. Station, Wilmslow.*

I have maintained an interest in aviation to this day.

When I left the RAF in 1950, I started work for Captain Ramsden at Swains Hill Farm. It was there that I met my future wife and we got married in 1952.

# Jean Silver

## My memories from 1935.

1935 I started school with my twin brother Donald at South Warnborough. Mrs Bowie the head teacher, who lived near us, took us to school on the first day. We didn't do much that day but make friends with the other children. I remember the lovely black stove fire in the middle of the room, it was so warm! From then on we went to school with our sister Joyce.

Every day on our way to school we had to pass Mrs Pearson's house, which was near the shop. Her bulldog was always sitting inside her gate and would run after us, because we were afraid of it!

1937 My father built a large dolls house for Joyce and me. We had lots of fun playing with our dolls and also dressing our kittens in dolls clothes, putting them in our pram and taking them for a walk in the garden. We also pretended we were grown up by wearing mum's shoes.

1938 We all attended Sunday school and I was given a hymn book by Rev. Oldfield, probably for good attendance. We went to church every Sunday morning.

Sunday evenings we would go for a long walk with Mum and Dad, up Westers Lane, coming out at Lasham and then on to The Golden Pot. There we would have a very welcome glass of lemonade and a packet of crisps before walking home past Powntley Copse.

1940 One day when we were at school, nine bombs fell, with one falling on the house next door where Ron and Reg Silver, my cousins lived. When we got home from school we were met by Mrs Pilkington, the Lady from the Manor House. She took us to her home and gave us tea and sweets.

Dad was called up into the Army. One day coming home from school we saw a plane which was German. It fired at us and we fell to the ground, but we were not hurt!

1941 One Sunday afternoon, a lot of tents were being put up in the field opposite our houses by the RAF Regiment. They were getting ready to move overseas.

1942 We were given time out of school to pick up potatoes 0n the local farms. The "Silver Kids" as we were called, that is Reg, Ron, Don, Joy and myself, played cricket in the field opposite. We also went scrumping in the Manor grounds! If I can recollect, if there was any kind of trouble in the village, one of us would get the blame!

At Christmas we all went carol singing at Powntley Copse, which was quite a long walk. In the spring we picked primroses, cowslips and bluebells and sold them to people in their cars passing through the village. The money went towards sandals for school.

For a time I was a Sunday school teacher and we met in the village hall. I read stories to the children from the scripture book.

1944 Here is a photo of me when I was 14 years old

1945 The Fire Service came to the village for a few weeks. Hoddington House at Upton Grey became a hospital for wounded Servicemen.

1946 I left school and worked at Dickers, the grocery store and then left to work at the NAFFI at RAF Odiham. Later, I went to work at Kelvins in Basingstoke.

1952 My brother Don got married this year and here we are together outside of our house on his wedding day.

I also got married to Stan in the same year and we had a son, Adrian, in 1956.

# Ron Silver

I was born on 3rd April 1927 at No. 4 Alton Rd. South Warnborough.

Here is a photo of our house with my Mum and my brother Reg, taken in the early thirties. It was the corner of the house, directly behind us that suffered during the bombing in 1940 and mentioned later.

In 1932 I started school at the village school, where Mrs. Bowie was the head teacher. My schooldays at South Warnborough were happy ones, where the whole school was in one big, airy classroom.

One instruction I remember well, very strange by today's standards, was the procedure to follow if we needed the toilets. These were situated at the end of the playground. As there was no running water, there was a very primitive ash system where pots containing ashes were emptied when a handle was pulled!

I cannot remember the age we left this school to go to Long Sutton School, but I think I was 8/9 years old (1935/36). I still have our photos from those days - typical school ones!

Reg. and me

We were taken to Long Sutton by Guy Freeman in his station wagon, and on many occasions, because of numbers, he had to make two journeys. We waited at our assembly point at the "Cross Tree" and during the winter months, we spent our time sliding on the village pond, which was opposite, but no longer there!

Our teachers at the school were the head, Mr. Wilmot with Miss Russ and Miss Hoyes. A Miss Bastar was the supply teacher.

I loved school and was always willing to assist in school activities. I enjoyed sport and always paid attention in lessons – well nearly always! Sometimes there would be a little snigger or sigh and the next moment Mr Wilmot would be leaning over your shoulder, then there would be lines or standing out in front of the class.

I left school at 14 years old and started work with A J Sapp & Sons in Basingstoke and had to cycle to and from the town every day. I worked as a carpenter with Bert Tubb and Jack Bishton. My first experience was working on army huts for a searchlight site situated at the far end of Westers Lane – the lane leading from S.W. to Humbly Grove, where Capt. Simpson lived.

The war came to us on the 24th October 1940, when in the morning at about 10am our house received a direct hit from one bomb of a stick of bombs. Fortunately, my mother who was in the house at the time, received only a few cuts and bruises. It was a miracle, considering our front door had been blown over the road into the field opposite our house! That is, in the field where the villagers played cricket and football.

We were only allowed to stay in our house on the first night and then we moved to The Lodge, owned by Mrs. McClean. Later, Reg. (my brother) and I moved to stay with Mr. Taylor, who lived in a bungalow next to the Police House in Gastons Lane. He was an older gentleman and was very kind to us. We were always sent to bed at a regular time with a candle and torch, together with a list of do's and don'ts - no noise and ensure no lights could be seen from outside! We naturally used to panic when the air raid warnings sounded!

At that time P.C. Chapman lived in the Police House with two sons and one daughter – Sid, Jim and Molly.

As time passed, I wondered what I could do next? So I joined the ATC, where we had one night a week at RAF Odiham. I eventually became a Corporal >>>>

Our Commanding Officer was Jack Southworth who lived in one of the bungalows in Wells Hill, next to the Goodchilds?

Later I served in the Local Defence Volunteers, later called the Home Guard, until I was called up. I was very keen on sport and played cricket for S.W. under the care of Dad, who encouraged both of us in the game. Dad was called Feller, the man with one hand and with a few tricks up his sleeve – (the artful codger!), but he could play cricket well – and he was also good at football.

We played in the field opposite the Council Houses, where cows were kept. The pitch was fenced off with barbed wire to keep them out, but we always had a bucket and spade to clean up any pats from cows that managed to get on to the pitch and also to clear the outfield.

Cricket was played every Saturday, but Reg. and I were only picked occasionally. Some of the team players were,

Percy Silver, Arthur Silver, R. Maynard
Ike Cripps, A. Cripps, Pimp Stacey, Bill Hope,
John Stacey, Bert Thomas, Bob Maynard,
Charley Kersley, Perce Pither.
- when needed, Reg & Ron Silver

I remember my life at home very well. We played many games, including cards – a favourite of mine! My Dad came up with an idea to enable us to play billiards on the kitchen table. A golf ball was used as the cue ball and spent cartridges placed on the table, to remain standing and not to be knocked down! – good fun! Other games were dominoes and darts, where the dart board was hung on the back of the door. My parents were very kind, but strict and we had to do as we were told.

In the early days we visited Hayling Island during the summer months, where my Uncle had donkeys on the beach. Reg & I helped by walking them up and down the beach at a penny or twopence a ride. We stayed down there for a while and were housed in a tent or caravan – it was good fun with plenty of laughs!

We had to "tighten our belts" prior to the 1939-45 war as there was very little money around. This photo shows the three of us after a session in our vegetable garden.

We were never without food during these times or during the war, as my Dad would go out with his ferrets and gun to catch rabbits or to shoot a pheasant. In those times we always helped each other, so the neighbours often benefited from his activities. My Dad's artificial "hand" is shining in the sun.

Here is a treasured photo of Dad with his cocker spaniel and ferrets, after he had been out to catch rabbits, with one of them from the day's bag!

We took our meals to school, consisting of sandwiches and a bun, but when rationing came in we had to be very careful. My Mother did a good job with the food and we never went without.

I had one or two hobbies, including collecting cigarette cards, mainly from Woodbine and Players cigarette packets. After nearly 70years, I still have sets of cards from those times.

A special photo of my Mum and Dad

Most of my family lived in the village –

Dad's sisters were Mrs Knight and Violet Silver (who lived in the bungalow opposite Mrs Pape in Lees Hill) and his brother who lived next door to us. In those days we all knew everybody in the village.

The people living in the South Warnborough council houses were,

No.1 Mrs Bowie, No.2 Mrs Hillyer
No.3 Mrs "Son" Silver, No. 4 Mrs P Silver
No.5 Mrs W Duce No. 6 Mrs Caplin

At the end of the row was The Never Despair garage, which had several owners – Mr. Dry, Mr. Richardson and Mr. Freeman.

The petrol pumps were initially manual, which meant the owner came out to turn the handle to give the ½ gallon or so – remembering that during the war it was strictly rationed! Later electric pumps were installed. Now of course, there is no petrol station

I remember quite a lot about the past village people and their homes, with many of the houses having since been replaced or removed completely.

The Green Garage, next to The Plough Inn, was owned by Mr Bedford and run by Owen Tyler. Nearby, were two cottages. Mrs Harris lived in one and Mrs Bristow in the other. There were also cottages near the village water pump, which was used for obtaining water for cattle.

I also remember the "cross tree", which had a stack pipe by the side of it and a hole at the bottom of the tree with a hollow trunk. We could climb up through the tree to the top. I did rescue my brother on one occasion and he never went inside again! The tree was a landmark and a meeting place, including a courting area.

There were always lots of troops in the area during wartime and we had the RAF Regiment in the cricket field opposite our homes. Within a short while they were on their way to Europe.

In March 1945 I was conscripted into the Army and went to Bodmin (on the moors) for four weeks initial training. I then went to Northampton for drafting abroad. We were put on a train to Dover, across the Channel at 4am, then through France and Switzerland to Taranto near the Adriatic coast of Italy. I was a little scared at being sent overseas, but I knew the conflict was nearly over.

Our troops were split up and I was put on a draft to Egypt, where I stayed for a short while at GHQ. At that time I was in the Duke of Cornwall's Light Infantry and here I am, looking smart, with a local mosque behind me.

During my time in Cairo, we were able take advantage and see many of the sites, including the pyramids at Giza. Here I am, with one of my mates on a highly decorated camel.

Later, I was on my way to Jerusalem via the Gazza Strip, to attend a promotion board, which I passed and which took me from Corporal to Sergeant.
On my return to Egypt I went to GHQ in FAYED and soon after was drafted to GHQ MELF in Athens, then moved on to Salonika in Northern Greece. Whilst there, I went to Turkey on a BMM mission for a two week period, which was quite long enough at that time!

I later returned to Greece and in 1949 I was put on demob release.

I had known quite a few lads when I had joined up, including Eddy Whiteland from Herriard, who was later discharged on medical grounds. I did meet him several times when I came home on leave, but eventually we lost touch. I got to know Bill Amor from Aldershot and we were together for a while. However I also lost touch with him after we got demobbed at Aldershot in 1949.

Our demob outfit – (civvies), consisted of a suit, shoes, socks, gloves, tie, 2 shirts and a raincoat or overcoat – finally a TRILBY, colour brown! I do believe this was about the last issue of civilian clothing.

I attended a wedding of one of the lads from the village, George Spreadborough, who married Joyce from Weston Patrick. The photo shows Joyce the bride and George, together with Ray and his wife Kate. On the right is Kate's brother Charlie, who had recently lost his fingers in an accident at a printing works, where he worked.

On my return to civilian life I got a job at Thornycroft, where I stayed for 24 years. I did have several jobs afterwards.

Whilst at Thornycroft, I met my lovely wife Valerie and we got married in 1955. We had 52 years together and enjoyed a wonderful married life.

I was a South Warnborough resident from 1927 to 1955, giving me 28 years in the village.

# Win. White

**M**y mother was born and grew up in South Warnborough. Here is her parents, (my grandparents) Mr. and Mrs. Thomas. He was the head gardener at The Manor and they lived in a semi-detached cottage right next to the Manor, (the one on the left).

Living "on the job" gave him problems during scrumping time when he had to deal directly with the village lads, including Ray Hillyer and his gang!

My brother Roland and I were born at Tunworth School House and my sister Doreen was born at our later home in Weston Corbett.

Here I am with my brother Roley – That day I was a bridesmaid.

Our father was eventually called up for the army and unfortunately was killed on active service in 1943.

We were then evicted from our home and for a time moved back to live with my Grandmother in South Warnborough.

We then moved into my Uncle Bert's cottage, who worked for Mrs. Gawne -still in the village - We stayed there until the Council were able to house us in one of the old NFS huts in Jan. 1947 and later we moved into the new Council Houses.

During this period my mother married Percy Helcoop and eventually my family grew with three stepsisters - Wendy, Dawn and ?? . All three were born in South Warnborough - Wendy was born at the old huts and Dawn at the Council Houses.

My working life in S. W. was first for Mrs. Bedford at the Police Cottage and then for the Rev. and Mrs. Harry Oldfield at the Rectory.

In 1950 I married Robert Gregory at St. Andrews Church, South Warnborough. Robert lived opposite the village school. After our marriage we lived at Owlesbury, near Winchester. However, we later moved back to the area for a short time - to Tile Barn between South Warnborough and Upton Grey. Both of our sons were christened at St. Andrews Church and one son started school at Long Sutton.

I realised that when we later moved to Hertfortshire that I seemed to be forever on the move! However, sometimes when I had a week off, I would return to South Warnborough to stay with my Mum. Then I loved to go to The Plough - now called The Poachers - to play darts with Tommy Goodchild. It was good fun with plenty of laughs!